9-25

OXFORD

CHOR
CLASSI

CW00546507

Christmas Motets

EDITED BY JOHN RUTTER

MUSIC DEPARTMENT

OXFORD
UNIVERSITY PRESS

OXFORD
UNIVERSITY PRESS

Great Clarendon Street, Oxford OX2 6DP, England
198 Madison Avenue, New York, NY10016, USA

Oxford University Press is a department of the University of Oxford.
It furthers the University's aim of excellence in research, scholarship,
and education by publishing worldwide in

Oxford New York
Athens Auckland Bangkok Bogotà Buenos Aires Calcutta
Cape Town Chennai Dar es Salaam Delhi Florence Hong Kong Istanbul
Karachi Kuala Lumpur Madrid Melbourne Mexico City Mumbai
Nairobi Paris São Paulo Singapore Taipei Tokyo Toronto Warsaw
with associated companies in Berlin Ibadan

First published 1999

3 5 7 9 10 8 6 4

ISBN 978-0-19-343704-3

Music originated on Sibelius

Printed in Great Britain on acid-free paper by
Halstan & Co. Ltd., Amersham, Bucks.

CONTENTS

Liturgical use: No. 1 is suitable for Advent. Nos. 2, 3, 4, 5, 6, 8, 9, 10, 11, 12, 13, 14, 15, and 16 are suitable for Christmas. Nos. 7 and 13 are suitable for Epiphany.

Instrumental parts are available on rental from the publisher for the following two items:

Scheidt: *In dulci jubilo*
2 trumpets in C; 3 trombones and tuba (or other suitable instruments) doubling Choir II. Organ plays from the vocal score.

Sweelinck: *Hodie Christus natus est*
Five parts (for strings, wind, or brass) doubling the voice parts, plus a continuo bass part. The two uppermost parts are shown for B flat and C instruments. A possible modern brass combination is 2 trumpets and 3 trombones. Organ or other keyboard continuo plays from the vocal score.

PREFACE

This collection of sixteen Christmas motets is a seasonal supplement to *European Sacred Music*, from which Oxford Choral Classics volume all Advent, Christmas, and Epiphany material was excluded to make room for a wider variety of other motets. The same guiding principles apply to this, as to all volumes in the series: to offer choirs a practical and inexpensive working library of standard repertoire in new, reliable editions and, where space allows, to include music which is less widely known but of special value within its genre. Editions are prepared from primary sources whenever possible; readily playable keyboard reductions are provided; translations (either for singing or study) are given for all texts not in English.

The term 'motet' has been freely interpreted to include seasonal vernacular compositions such as Mendelssohn's splendid *Frohlocket, ihr Völker auf Erden*, Cui's wonderfully rich and fervent *Magnificat*, and the ever-delightful *Riu, riu, chiu*. Four familiar carol-based pieces were likewise impossible to leave out: Hieronymus Praetorius's and Samuel Scheidt's contrasted eight-voice treatments of *In dulci jubilo*, Handl's lilting *Resonet in laudibus*, and the lovely *Quem pastores laudavere* of Michael Praetorius. The chronological range of this volume is from 1518, the year of Mouton's peerless *Nesciens mater*, to the eve of World War I, when Cui's *Magnificat*, one of the last and finest pre-revolutionary flowerings of Russian church music, was written; the geographical spread is from Spain to St Petersburg. Inevitably, the mainstay of any motet volume will be the great corpus of Renaissance polyphony, and the problem confronting the editor is what to select when so much is of high quality. I have not discriminated against music in more than four parts: some of the most imaginative and effective choral writing of the period would be thereby ruled out. Nor have I avoided including more than one setting of the same text, because there are good programme-building possibilities in juxtaposing different composers' treatments of the same words. Liturgically, Advent, Christmas, and Epiphany are all covered, and two substantial pieces (Bruckner's *Virga Jesse floruit* and the Cui *Magnificat*) are also suitable for use at other times of the year.

In a collection intentionally limited to 128 pages, there are inevitably many notable omissions, some of which it is hoped to rectify in a second volume. But every one of the sixteen pieces in this book is, I believe, well worth performing either in a church or concert context, and can provide valuable contrast and substance in programmes built mainly around carols.

Editorial practice

This is fully set out in the preface to *European Sacred Music*. Standard conventions have been followed, with the exception that editorially completed text underlay has not been italicized, and indications of ligature and coloration are omitted. Syllabic slurs in voice parts, as used in modern publishing style, have not generally been added. Beaming and stemming of notes have been modernized, as have spelling, capitalization, and punctuation of texts. Editorial suggestions of tempo and dynamics for pre-1700 pieces are generally included in the keyboard reductions. Acknowledgement is made to individuals (notably my associate editor for the series, Clifford Bartlett) and to libraries who provided microfilms and photocopies of items in this volume. We are grateful for their permission to use or consult their sources.

JOHN RUTTER

1. Virga Jesse floruit

(*Out of Jesse springs a flower*)

Alleluia verse at Feasts of the Virgin Mary
English version by John Rutter

ANTON BRUCKNER
(1824–96)

Alla breve, feierlich langsam [Solemn, slow]

13
cresc. sempre
ff
vir - ga Jes - se, vir - ga Jes - se flo - - - - - ru - it:
out of Jes - se, out of Jes - se springs a flow'r:
[p] cresc. sempre
20
ff sempre
Vir - - go De - - - - - um et ho - mi - nem
Lo, by God's will a vir - gin hath

27
ge - nu - it, Vir - go De-um et ho - mi-nem ge - nu-it:
brought forth, lo, a vir-gin hath brought forth Em - ma - nu-el:
ge - nu - it, Vir - go De-um et ho - mi-nem ge - nu-it:
brought forth, lo, a vir-gin hath brought forth Em - ma - nu-el:
ge - nu - it, Vir - go De-um et ho - mi-nem ge - nu-it:
brought forth, lo, a vir-gin hath brought forth Em - ma - nu-el:
ge - nu - it, Vir - go De-um et ho - mi-nem ge - nu-it:
brought forth, lo, a vir-gin hath brought forth Em - ma - nu-el:
34
pp cresc. mf cresc.
pa - cem De - us red - di-dit, pa - cem De - us
peace on earth, good will to men, peace on earth, good
pp cresc. [p] cresc. mf cresc.
pa - cem, pa - cem, pa - cem De - us red - di-dit, pa-cem,
peace on earth, peace on earth, good will to men, peace on
pp cresc. cresc. mf cresc.
pa - cem De - us red - di-dit, pa - cem, pa - cem De - us
peace on earth, good will to men, peace on earth, on earth, good
p [cresc.] mf
pa - cem De - us red - di-dit,
peace on earth, good will to men,
pp cresc. p cresc. mf cresc.

41
ff
cresc.
fff
red - di-dit, pa - cem, pa - cem
will to men, glo - ry, glo - ry
f
cresc.
[>]
pa - cem De - us red - di-dit, pa-cem, pa - cem
earth, good will, good will to men, glo-ry, glo - ry
red - di-dit, pa-cem, pa - cem, pa - cem
will to men, glo-ry, glo - ry, glo - ry
pa - cem De - us red - di-dit, pa - cem
peace on earth, good will to men, glo - ry
48
pp
De - us red - di - dit, in se, in se,
in the high - est heav'n. Be - hold, be - hold,
De - us red - di - dit, in se, in
in the high - est heav'n. Be - hold, be -

56
cresc. mf cresc. dim.
in se re-con - ci - li - ans i - ma sum -
be - hold, ev - 'ry val - ley shall be ex - alt -
se, in se re-con - ci - li - ans i - ma sum -
- hold, be - hold, ev - 'ry val - ley shall be ex - alt -
63
ff fff
-mis. Al - le - lu - ia, al - le - lu - ia, al - le - lu - ia,
- ed.
Al - le - lu - ia, al - le - lu - ia, al - le -
[p] dim.
p dim.

69
pp
dim.
al - le - lu - ia, al - le - lu - - - - - - - - - - -
pp
dim.
al - le - lu - ia, al - le - lu - - - - - - - - - - -
pp
dim.
al - le - lu - ia, al - le - lu - - - - - - - - - - -
pp
dim.
- lu - ia, al - le - lu - - - - - - - - - - -
pp
dim.
75
fff
- ia, al - le - lu - ia, al - le - lu - - -
ff
fff
- ia, al - le - lu - ia, al - le - lu - - - ia, al - le - lu - - -
ff
[fff]
- ia, al - le - lu - - ia, al - le - lu - ia, al - le - lu - - -
ff
fff
- ia, al - le - lu - - ia, al - le - lu - - - ia, al - le - lu - - -
ff
fff

81
pp
p
ia, al - le - lu
ia, al - le - lu - ia, al - le - lu - ia,
mf
ia, al - le - lu - ia, al - le - lu - ia, al - le - lu - ia, al - le-
ia, al - le - lu -
86
mf
[dim.]
p dim. sempre
ppp
al - le - lu - ia.
falsetto
f
dim.
-lu - ia, al - le - lu - ia, al - le - lu - ia, al - le - lu - ia.
cresc.
[dim.]
- ia, al - le - lu - ia.

2. O magnum mysterium

(*O marvel and mystery*)

Christmas Day
John Rutter

WILLIAM BYRD
(1543–1623)

9
- mi - ra - bi - le, et ad - mi - ra - bi - le sa - - cra - men -
- drous sa - cra - ment, and won - drous sa - cra - ment O most ho -
et ad - mi - ra - bi - le sa - - cra - men - -
and won - drous sa - cra - ment O most ho - -
- le sa - cra - men - - - - tum, et ad - mi -
- ment O most ho - - - - ly, and won - drous
- bi - le sa - - - cra - men - tum, sa - cra - men - tum,
- cra - ment O most ho - - ly, O most ho - - ly,
13
-tum, sa - cra - men - tum, et ad - mi - ra - bi - le sa -
- ly, O most ho - ly, and won - drous sa - cra - ment O
-tum, sa - cra - men - - tum, et ad - mi - ra - - bi - le sa -
- ly, O most ho - - - ly, and won - drous sa - cra - ment O
- ra - bi - le sa - - cra - men - tum, et ad - mi - ra - bi - le
sa - cra - ment O most ho - ly, and won - drous sa - cra - ment
et ad - mi - ra - bi - le sa - cra - men - tum, sa - -
and won - drous sa - cra - ment O most ho - ly, O
cresc.
mf

17
- cra - men - tum, ut a - ni - ma - li - a, ut
most ho - ly, that in a hum - ble crib, that
- cra-men - - tum, ut a - ni - ma - li - a, ut a - ni -
most ho - - ly, that in a hum - ble crib, that in a
sa - cra-men - tum, ut a - ni - ma - li - a, ut a - ni - ma - li - a
O most ho - - ly, that in a hum - ble crib, that in a hum - ble crib
- cra - men - tum, ut a - ni - ma - li - a vi - de -
most ho - ly, that in a hum - ble crib, a hum -
dim.
p
mp
22
a - ni - ma - li - a vi - de - - rent Do - mi-num na - - -
in a hum - ble crib the ox and ass should see our
- ma - li - a vi - de - rent Do - mi - num, ut a - ni - ma - li - a vi -
hum - ble crib the ox and ass should see, that in a crib the ox and
vi - de - rent Do - mi - num na - - tum, na -
the ox and ass should see our Lord, our
- - rent, ut a - ni - ma - li - a vi - de - - rent
- ble crib, that in a hum - ble crib the ox and
cresc.
mf

26
-tum, vi - de - rent Do - mi-num na - - - tum, na -
Lord, should see our Lord and our Sa - - - viour, our
- de - rent Do - mi - num, vi - de - rent Do - mi-num na - tum, na -
ass should see our Lord and Sa - viour, should see our Lord and Sa -
- - tum, vi - de - rent Do - mi - num na - - - tum, ja -
Lord, should see our Lord and our Sa - - - viour a -
Do - mi - num, vi - de - rent Do - mi - num na - tum, ja -
ass should see, should see our Lord and our Sa - viour a -
dim.
p
pp
30
- - - tum, ja - cen - tem in prae - se - pi - o, ja - cen - tem
Sa - - viour a - mong them in the sta - ble laid, a - mong them
- tum, ja - cen - tem in prae - se - pi - o, in prae - se - - - pi -
-viour a - mong them in the sta - ble laid, in the sta - - - ble
- cen - tem in prae - se - pi - o, ja - cen - tem in prae - se - pi -
- mong them in the sta - ble laid, a - mong them in the sta - ble
-cen - tem in prae - se - pi - o, in prae - se - pi - o, ja -
-mong them in the sta - ble laid, in the sta - ble laid, a -
p

* Bars 45–75 are printed in the *Gradualia* as a separate motet, *Beata Virgo*, which may follow straight on in performance from *O magnum mysterium* to good effect. However, either motet may of course be performed separately.

Beata Virgo

45
Be - a - - ta Vir - go, cu - jus vi - sce-ra
Most bless - ed Vir - gin, who in pu - ri - ty
Be - a - ta Vir - - go, cu - jus vi - - sce -
Most bless - ed Vir - gin, who in pu - - ri -
Be - a - - ta Vir - go, cu - jus vi - sce-
Most bless - ed Vir - gin, who in pu - ri-
Be - a - ta Vir - - go, cu - jus vi - sce-
Most bless - ed Vir - gin, who in pu - ri-
p
cresc.

51
me - ru - e - runt por - ta - - - re, por - ta - -
bore by God's will our Sa - - - viour, our Sa - -
- ra me - ru - e - - runt por - ta - - re, por - ta - re Do -
- ty bore by God's will our Sa - - viour, our Sa - viour Je -
- ra me - ru - e - - - runt por - ta - - - re Do - mi -
- ty bore by God's will our Sa - - - viour Je - sus
- ra me - - ru - e - runt por - ta - - re, por - ta -
- ty bore by God's will our Sa - - viour, our Sa -
mp
cresc.

* This section may be sung by three solo voices to good effect.

65
S.
-a, a - - - - - - ve Ma - ri - - a,
-ry, hail, Vir - gin Ma - - ry,
A.
Ma - ri - - - - a, Ma - ri - a, gra - ti - a ple - na, gra -
hail, Vir - - - gin Ma - ry, full of grace art thou, full
T.
- - ve Ma - ri - - a, Ma - ri - - - a, gra - ti - a
Vir - gin Ma - - ry, hail, Ma - - - ry, full of grace
cresc.
mp
69
gra - ti - a ple - - na, Do - mi-nus te - cum,
full of grace art thou: God is with thee,
- ti - a ple - - - - - - - na, Do - mi-nus te - cum, Do -
of grace art thou: God is with thee, God
ple - - - - - na, Do - mi-nus te - cum, Do -
art thou: God is with thee, God
mf
72
D.S. al Fine
(back to p. 13)
te - - - cum, Do - mi-nus te - - - - - - - cum.
with thee, God is with thee.
- mi-nus te - cum, Do - mi-nus te - - - - - - - cum.
is with thee, God is with thee.
- mi-nus te - - - - - - cum, te - - - - cum.
is with thee, with thee.
cresc.
f dolce
dim.
mp

3. Magnificat

(*The Lord be exalted and magnified*)

Canticle of the Blessed Virgin Mary
Transliteration by Bruce Hamilton
English version by John Rutter

CÉSAR CUI (1835–1918)
Op. 93

* Notes lower than this D flat in the bottom bass part are always doubled an octave higher and may be omitted.
† The solo part is equally suitable for mezzo-soprano.
The symbol ŏ in the transliteration indicates a sound nearer to 'a' than to 'o'.

9
S.
byez srav - nye - ni - ya se - ra - fim, byez ist - lye - ni - ya Bo - ga Slo - va rozhd - shu - yu,
se - ra - phim in the realm of light, bless - ed Mo - ther and mai - den, thou who bore our Lord,
A.
byez srav - nye - ni - ya se - ra - fim, byez ist - lye - ni - ya Bo - ga Slo - va rozhd - shu - yu,
se - ra - phim in the realm of light, bless - ed Mo - ther and mai - den, thou who bore our Lord,
T.
p
Byez ist - lye - ni - ya Bo - ga Slo - va rozhd - shu - yu,
Bless - ed Mo - ther and mai - den, thou who bore our Lord,
B.
p
Slo - va rozhd - shu - yu,
Thou who bore our Lord,
Tya vye - li - cha - - yem.
A - ve Ma - ri - - a.
14
f
su - shchu - yu Bŏ - gŏ - ro - dit - su Tya vye - li - cha - yem.
sin - less and pure and un - de - filed, A - ve Ma - ri - a.
su - shchu - yu Bŏ - gŏ - ro - dit - su Tya vye - li - cha - yem.
sin - less and pure and un - de - filed, A - ve Ma - ri - a.
su - shchu - yu Bŏ - gŏ - ro - dit - su Tya vye - li - cha - yem.
sin - less and pure and un - de - filed, A - ve Ma - ri - a.
su - shchu - yu Bŏ - gŏ - ro - dit - su Tya vye - li - cha - yem.
sin - less and pure and un - de - filed, A - ve Ma - ri - a.
Ped. *

Tempo I
Solo
S.
A.
T.
B.
Ya - ko pri - zrye na smi - rye - ni - ye ra - byi Svo - ye - ya, sye bo ŏt - nyi - nye u - bla -
He hath re - gard - ed the low - li - ness of his hand - maid, and be - hold, all ge - ne -
Tya vye - li - cha - yem,
A - ve Ma - ri - a,
Tya vye - li -
A - ve Ma -
Poco più mosso
- zhat mya vsi ro - di.
- ra - tions shall call me bless - ed.
vye - li - cha - yem.
Ma - ri - a.
Chest - nyei - shu - yu khe - ru - vim i
A - bove all the che - ru - bim, more
- cha - yem.
- ri - a.
Chest - nyei - shu - yu khe - ru -
A - bove the che - ru -

28
S.
A.
T.
B.
p
Byez ist - lye - ni - ya Bo - ga
Bless - ed Mo-ther and mai - den,
slav - nyei - shu - yu byez srav - nye - ni - ya se - ra - fim, byez ist - lye - ni - ya Bo - ga
glo - rious than the se - ra - phim in the realm of light, bless - ed Mo-ther and mai - den,
- vim, byez ist - lye - ni - ya Bo - ga
- bim, bless - ed, bless - ed Mo - ther,
32
mf
f
Slo - va rozhd - shu - yu, su - shchu - yu Bŏ - gŏ - ro - dit - su Tya vye - li -
thou who bore our Lord, sin - less and pure and un - de - filed, A - ve Ma -
Slo - va rozhd - shu - yu, Bŏ - gŏ - ro - dit - su Tya vye - li -
thou who bore our Lord, pure and un - de - filed, A - ve Ma -

Tempo I
37
Solo
S.
A.
T.
B.
mf
pp
Ya-ko sŏ-tvŏ-ri mnye vye-li-chi-ye Sil-nyi, i
He that is migh-ty hath mag-ni-fied me, and
-cha - - yem.
-ri - - - a.
Tya vye - - li -
A - - ve Ma -
Tempo I
42
svya-tŏ i-mya Ye-go, i mi-lŏst Ye-go vro-dyi rŏ-dov bŏ-ya-shchim-ssya Ye -
ho-ly is his Name: his mer-cy is sure un-to his peo-ple through-out all ge-ne -
-cha - yem, Tya vye - li - cha - - - - - - -
-ri - a, a - - - - ve Ma - ri - - - - - - - -
vye - li - cha - - - - - - -
A-ve Ma - ri - - - - - - -
3

46
Poco più mosso
- go.
- ra - tions.
mf
- yem. Chest - nyei - shu - yu khe - ru - vim i slav - nyei - shu - yu
- a. A - bove all the che - ru - bim, more glo - rious than the
- yem. Chest - nyei - shu - yu khe - ru - vim i slav - nyei - shu - yu
- a. A - bove all the che - ru - bim, more glo - rious than the
- yem. Chest - nyei - shu - yu khe - ru - vim i slav - nyei -
- a. A - bove all the che - ru - bim, more glo - rious
(B.1)
- yem. Chest - nyei - shu - yu khe - ru - vim i slav - nyei -
- a. A - bove all the che - ru - bim, more glo - rious
Poco più mosso
50
S.
byez srav - nye - ni - ya se - ra - fim, Bo - ga Slo - va
se - ra - phim in the realm of light, thou who bore, who
A.
byez srav - nye - ni - ya se - ra - fim, byez ist - lye - ni - ya Bo - ga Slo - va
se - ra - phim in the realm of light, bless - ed Mo - ther and mai - den, thou who
T.
- shu - yu se - ra - fim, byez ist - lye - ni - ya Bo - ga Slo - va
than the se - ra - phim, bless - ed Mo - ther and mai - den, thou who
B.
- shu - yu se - ra - fim, byez ist - lye - ni - ya
than the se - ra - phim, bless - ed Mo - ther and

54
rozhd - shu - yu, su - shchu - yu Bŏ - gŏ - ro - dit - su Tya vye - li - cha -
bore our Lord, sin - less and pure and un - de - filed, A - ve Ma - ri -
rozhd - shu - yu, Bŏ - gŏ - ro - dit - su Tya vye - li - cha - yem,
bore our Lord, pure and un - de - filed, A - ve Ma - ri - a,
rozhd - shu - yu, su - shchu - yu Bŏ - gŏ - ro - dit - su Tya vye - li - cha -
bore our Lord, sin - less and pure and un - de - filed, A - ve Ma - ri -
Bo - ga Slo - va rozhd - shu - yu Tya vye - li - cha -
mai - den, pure and un - de - filed, A - ve Ma - ri -
60
Tempo I
Solo
S.
A.
T.
B.
Sŏ - tvŏ - ri dyer - zha - vu myish - tsye - yu Svŏ - ye - yu,
With his own right arm hath God dis - played his pow - er:
yem, vye - li - cha - yem,
a. A - ve Ma - ri - a,
vye - li - cha - yem, vye - li - cha - yem,
a - ve Ma - ri - a. A - ve Ma - ri - a,
yem, vye - li - cha - yem,
a. A - ve Ma - ri - a,
yem, vye - li - cha - yem,
a. A - ve Ma - ri - a,
Tempo I

66
ra - stŏ - chi gor - dyi - ya myi - sli - yu syerd - tsa yikh.
He hath scat - tered all the proud in their va - ni - ty.
vye - li - cha - yem. Chest -
a - ve Ma - ri - a. A -
vye - li - cha - yem. Chest -
a - ve Ma - ri - a. A -
vye - li - cha - yem.
a - ve Ma - ri - a.
vye - li - cha - yem.
a - ve Ma - ri - a.
70 Poco più mosso
S.
A.
T.
B.
- nyei - shu - yu khe - ru - vim i slav - nyei - shu - yu byez srav - nye - ni - ya se - ra -
- bove all the che - ru - bim, more glo - rious than the se - ra - phim in the realm of
- nyei - shu - yu khe - ru - vim i slav - nyei - shu - yu byez srav - nye - ni - ya se - ra -
- bove all the che - ru - bim, more glo - rious than the se - ra - phim in the realm of
Byez ist -
Bless - ed
Byez ist - lye - ni - ya,
Bless - ed Mo - ther and
Poco più mosso

74
S.
f
-fim, byez ist - lye - ni - ya Bo - ga Slo - va rozhd - shu - yu, su - shchu-
light, bless - ed Mo - ther and mai - den, thou who bore our Lord, pure and
A.
f
-fim, byez ist - lye - ni - ya Bo - ga Slo - va rozhd - shu - yu, su - shchu-
light, bless - ed Mo - ther and mai - den, thou who bore our Lord, pure and
T.
f
-lye - ni - ya Bo - ga Slo - va rozhd - shu - yu, su - shchu-
Mo - ther and mai - den, thou who bore our Lord, pure and
B. 1
f
byez ist - lye - ni - ya Bo - ga Slo - va rozhd - shu - yu, su - shchu - yu
mai - den, Mo - ther and mai - den, thou who bore our Lord, pure and sin -
2
[p]
f
Bo - ga Slo - va rozhd - shu - yu, su - shchu - yu
Mai - den, thou who bore our Lord, pure and sin -
f
81
p
-yu Bŏ - gŏ - ro - dit - su Tya vye - li - cha - yem.
sin - less and un - de - filed, A - ve Ma - ri - a.
p
-yu Bŏ - gŏ - ro - dit - su Tya vye - li - cha - yem.
sin - less and un - de - filed, A - ve Ma - ri - a.
p
-yu Bŏ - gŏ - ro - dit - su Tya vye - li - cha - yem.
sin - less and un - de - filed, A - ve Ma - ri - a.
p
Bŏ - gŏ - ro - dit - su vye - li - cha - yem.
-less and un - de - filed, A - ve Ma - ri - a.
p
Bŏ - gŏ - ro - dit - su vye - li - cha - yem.
-less and un - de - filed, A - ve Ma - ri - a.
p

* In the source (score and parts) the alto and tenor parts from here to the first beat of bar 96 appear in the soprano and alto staves, probably a printer's error.

100
blag,
filled,
f
i bŏ - ga - tya - shchi - ya - ssya ŏt - pu -
and the rich he hath sent
pp
is - pol - nyi blag,
yea, he hath filled,
blag, is - pol - nyi blag,
filled, yea, he hath filled,
blag,
filled,
mf
Bŏ - ga - tya - - shchi - ya -
and the rich he hath
106
[Poco più mosso]
- sti tshchi.
emp - ty,
Chest - nyei - shu - yu
A - bove all the
ŏt - - pu - sti tshchi.
emp - - ty a - way.
Byez
Bless -
- ssya ŏt - - pu - sti tshchi.
sent emp - - ty a - way.

113
S.
A.
T.
B.
khe - ru - vim i slav - nyei - shu - yu byez srav - nye - ni - ya se - ra - fim, byez ist -
che - ru - bim, more glo - rious than the se - ra - phim in the realm of light, bless - ed
khe - ru - vim i slav - nyei - shu - yu byez srav - nye - ni - ya se - ra - fim, byez ist -
che - ru - bim, more glo - rious than the se - ra - phim in the realm of light, bless - ed
ist - - - - lye - - - - ni - - - - ya Bo - ga
- ed Mo - - - - ther and mai - den,
mf
Byez ist - lye - ni - ya
Bless - ed Mo - ther,
117
- lye - ni - ya Bo - ga Slo - va rozhd - shu - yu, su - shchu - yu Bŏ - gŏ -
Mo - ther and mai - den, thou who bore our Lord, pure and sin - less and
- lye - ni - ya Bo - - ga Slo - va rozhd - shu - yu, su - shchu - yu Bŏ - gŏ -
Mo - ther and mai - - den, thou who bore our Lord, pure and sin - less and
Slo - - - - va rozhd - shu - yu, su - shchu - yu Bŏ - gŏ -
Mo - - - - ther and mai - den, pure and sin - less and
Bo - - - ga Slo - va rozhd - shu - yu, su - shchu - yu Bŏ - gŏ -
Mo - - - - ther and mai - den, pure and sin - less and

122
Tempo I
Solo
Vŏs - pri -
For be -
S.
A.
T.
B.
f
mf
- ro - dit - su
un - de - filed,
Tya vye - li - cha - yem,
A - ve Ma - ri - a,
Tempo I
128
- yat Iz - ra - i - lya, ot - rŏ - ka Svo - ye - go, po - mya - nu - ti mi - lo - sti,
- hold, the gra - cious and mer - ci - ful Lord de - fend - eth his ser - vant Is - ra - el,
pp
vye - li - cha -
a - ve Ma - ri -
3

132
ya - ko - zhe gla - go - la kŏ ŏt - tsyem na - shim, Av - ra - a - mu i
e - ven as he pro - mised un - to our fa - thers, un - to A - bra - ham, and
-yem, vye - li - cha
- a, a - ve Ma
136
ri - te - nu - to
Più mosso
sye - mye - ni ye - go da - zhe dŏ vye - ka.
un - to all his seed, now and for ev - er.
yem.
ri - a.
Chest - nyei - shu - yu khe - ru - vim i
A - bove all the che - ru - bim, more

141
S.
slav - nyei - shu - yu byez srav - nye - ni - ya se - ra - fim, byez ist - lye - ni - ya Bo - ga
glo - rious than the se - ra - phim in the realm of light, bless - ed Mo-ther and mai - den,
A.
slav - nyei - shu - yu byez srav - nye - ni - ya se - ra - fim, byez ist - lye - ni - ya Bo - ga
glo - rious than the se - ra - phim in the realm of light, bless - ed Mo-ther and mai - den,
T.
slav - nyei - shu - yu byez srav - nye - ni - ya se - ra - fim, byez ist - lye - ni - ya Bo - ga
glo - rious than the se - ra - phim in the realm of light, bless - ed Mo-ther and mai - den,
B.
slav - nyei - shu - yu byez srav - nye - ni - ya se - ra - fim, byez ist - lye - ni - ya
glo - rious than the se - ra - phim in the realm of light, bless - ed Mo - ther,

145
f
p
Slo - va rozhd - shu - yu, su - shchu - yu Bŏ - gŏ - ro - dit - su, Bŏ - gŏ -
thou who bore our Lord, sin - less and pure and un - de - filed, pure and
Slo - va rozhd - shu - yu, Bŏ - gŏ - ro - dit - su, Bŏ - gŏ - ro - dit -
thou who bore our Lord, pure and un - de - filed, pure and un - de -
Slo - va rozhd - shu - yu, su - shchu - yu Bŏ - gŏ - ro - dit - su, Bŏ - gŏ -
thou who bore our Lord, sin - less, pure and un - de - filed, pure and
[p]
Bo - ga rozhd - shu - yu, su - shchu - yu Bŏ - gŏ - ro - dit -
thou who bore our Lord, sin - less and pure and un - de -

151
Solo
S.
A.
T.
B.
f
Vye - li - chit du - sha mŏ - ya,
The Lord be ex - alt - ed,
- ro - dit - su Tya vye - li - cha - - yem, vye - li - cha -
un - de - filed, A - ve Ma - ri - - a, a - ve Ma - ri -
- su vye - li - cha - - yem, vye - li - cha -
- filed, A - ve Ma - ri - - a, Ma - ri -
- ro - dit - su Tya vye - li - cha - - yem, vye - li - cha -
un - de - filed, A - ve Ma - ri - - a, a - ve Ma - ri -
- su
- filed,
f
157
vye - li - chit Go - spŏ - da.
ex - alt - ed and mag - ni - fied.
[cresc.]
[f]
- yem. Chest - nyei - shu - yu khe - ru - vim i slav - nyei -
- a. A - bove all the che - ru - bim, more glo - rious
[cresc.]
[f]
- yem. Chest - nyei - shu - yu khe - ru - vim i slav - nyei -
- a. A - bove all the che - ru - bim, more glo - rious
[cresc.]
[f]
- yem. Chest - nyei - shu - yu khe - ru - vim i slav - nyei -
- a. A - bove all the che - ru - bim, more glo - rious
f
Slav - nyei - shu - yu byez srav - nye -
more glo - rious, more glo - rious, glo - rious
[cresc.]
f

164
S.
A.
T.
B.
p
mf
-shchu - yu se - ra - fim, Tya vye - li - cha - yem,
than the se - ra - phim, A - ve Ma - ri - a,
-shchu - yu se - ra - fim, Tya vye - li - cha
than the se - ra - phim, A - ve Ma - ri -
vye - li -
Ma - ri -
- ni - ya se - ra - fim,
172
poco ritardando
f
[p]
vye - li - cha - yem, vye - li - cha - yem.
Ma - ri - a, a - ve Ma - ri - a.
-yem, vye - li - cha - yem, vye - li - cha - yem.
- a, Ma - ri - a, a - ve Ma - ri - a.
-cha - yem, Tya vye - li - cha - yem.
- a, a - a - ve Ma - ri - a.
- a,
Ped.

4. Quem vidistis, pastores?

(*Shepherds, tell, whom have you seen?*)

Antiphon at Lauds for Christmas Day
English translation by John Rutter

RICHA[illegible]
([illegible]550)

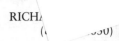

S.
ter - ris quis ap - pa - ru - it?
mar - vel has ap - peared on earth?
- pa - - - ru - it?
- peared on earth?
A.
ter - ris quis ap - pa - ru - it?
mar - vel has ap - peared on earth?
T.
Na - tum vi - di - mus, Na - tum
We have seen a Child, Christ the
Na - tum vi - di - mus, Na - tum
We have seen a Child, Christ the
B.
Na - tum vi - di - mus, Na - tum
We have seen a Child, Christ the
legato
13
S.
Na - tum
We have
Na - tum
We have
A.
Na - tum
We have
T.
vi - di - mus, et cho - ros an - ge - lo - rum, Na - tum
Ho - ly One, with choirs of an - gel voi - ces, we have
vi - di - mus, et cho - ros an - ge - lo - rum, Na - tum
Ho - ly One, with choirs of an - gel voi - ces, we have
B.
vi - di - mus, et cho - ros an - ge - lo - rum, Na - tum
Ho - ly One, with choirs of an - gel voi - ces, we have
f

19
S.
vi - di - mus, Na - tum vi - - di - mus, et cho - ros an - ge -
seen a Child, Christ the Ho - - ly One, with choirs of an - gel
vi - di - mus, Na - - tum vi - - di - mus, et
seen a Child, Christ the Ho - - ly One, with
A.
vi - di - mus, Na - - tum vi - - di - mus, et
seen a Child, Christ the Ho - - ly One, with
T.
vi - di - mus, Na - tum vi - - di - mus, et cho - ros an - ge -
seen a Child, Christ the Ho - - ly One, with choirs of an - gel
vi - di - mus, Na - - tum vi - - di - mus, et
seen a Child, Christ the Ho - - ly One, with
B.
vi - di - mus, Na - - tum vi - - di - mus, et cho - ros an - ge -
seen a Child, Christ the Ho - - ly One, with choirs of an - gel
25
S.
-lo - rum, et cho - ros an - ge - lo - - - - - - - - rum
voi - ces, with choirs of an - gel voi - - - - - - - - ces
cho - ros an - ge - lo - rum, et cho - ros an - ge - lo - - - - rum
choirs of an - gel voi - ces, with choirs of an - gel voi - - - - ces
A.
cho - ros an - ge - lo - rum, et cho - ros an - ge - lo - - - - rum
choirs of an - gel voi - ces, with choirs of an - gel voi - - - - ces
T.
-lo - rum, et cho-ros an-ge-lo - - - - - - rum
voi - ces, with choirs of an-gel voi - - - - - - ces
cho - ros an - ge - lo - rum, et cho - ros an - ge - lo - - - - rum
choirs of an - gel voi - ces, with choirs of an - gel voi - - - - ces
B.
-lo - rum, et cho - ros an - ge - lo - - - - - - - - - rum
voi - ces, with choirs of an - gel voi - - - - - - - - - ces

* Original time signature **3** . Notes values in this section quartered.

42
S.
col - lau - dan - - tes Do - mi - num,
sing-ing in praise to the Lord,
col - lau - dan - - tes Do - mi - num,
sing-ing in praise to the Lord,
A.
-num, col - lau - dan - - tes Do - mi - num,
Lord, sing-ing in praise to the Lord,
T.
-num, Do - mi - num, Do - mi - num,
Lord, sing - ing in praise to the Lord,
-num, col - lau - dan - tes Do - mi - num, col - lau - dan-tes Do - mi - num,
Lord, sing-ing in praise to the Lord, to the glo - ry of the Lord,
B.
-num, col - lau - dan - - tes Do - mi - num,
Lord, sing-ing in praise to the Lord,
47
S.
col - - lau - dan - - tes Do - - - - mi - num.
to the glo - - - ry of the Lord.
col - - lau - dan - - tes Do - - mi - - num.
to the glo - - - ry of the Lord.
A.
col - - lau - dan - - tes Do - - mi - - num.
to the glo - - - ry of the Lord.
T.
col - - lau - dan - tes Do - - - - - mi - num.
to the glo - ry of the Lord.
col - - lau - dan - - tes Do - - - mi - num.
to the glo - - - ry of the Lord.
B.
col - - lau - dan - - tes Do - - - mi - num.
to the glo - - - ry of the Lord.
f

54
S.
Al-le-lu-ia, al-le-lu-ia, al - le - lu - ia, al-le-lu-ia, al-le-lu-ia,
Al-le-lu-ia, al-le-lu-ia, al-le-lu-ia, al-le - lu - ia, al-le-lu-ia, al-le-lu-ia,
A.
Al-le-lu-ia, al-le-lu-ia, al - le-lu - ia, al-le-lu-ia, al-le-lu-ia,
T.
Al-le-lu-ia, al-le-lu-ia, al - le-lu - ia,
Al-le-lu-ia, al-le-lu-ia, al-le-lu - - ia,
B.
Al-le-lu-ia, al-le-lu-ia, al - le-lu - ia,
mp leggiero
59
S.
al - le - lu - ia, al - le - lu - ia,
al - le - lu - - ia, al - le - lu - ia, al - le - lu -
A.
al - le - lu - ia, al - le - lu - ia, al - le - lu - ia,
T.
al - le - lu - ia, al - le - lu - ia, al - le - lu - - - ia,
al - le - lu - ia, al - le - lu - ia, al - le - lu - - ia, al - le - lu - ia,
B.
al - le - lu - ia, al - le - lu - ia, al - le - lu - - ia,
cresc.

63
S.
al - le - lu - ia, al - le - lu - - - ia, al - le - lu - ia, al - le - lu - - -
- ia, al - le - lu - ia, al - le - lu - ia, al - le - lu - ia, al - le - lu -
A.
al - le - lu - ia, al - le - lu - - ia,
T.
al - le - lu - ia, al - le - lu - ia, al - le - lu - - -
al - le - lu - ia, al - le - lu - - ia, al - le - lu - ia, al - le - lu -
B.
al - le - lu - ia, al - le - lu - ia, al - le - lu - - ia, al - le - lu - ia,
mf
cresc.
f
67
S.
- ia, al - le - lu - ia, al - le - lu - ia, al - - le - - - lu - ia.
- ia, al - le - lu - ia, al - - - - le - - lu - - ia.
A.
al - le - lu - ia, al - le - lu - ia, al - le - lu - ia.
T.
- ia, al - le - lu - ia, al - le - lu - ia, al - - le - lu - ia.
- ia, al - le - lu - ia, al - le - lu - ia, al - le - lu - ia.
B.
al - le - lu - ia, al - le - lu - ia, al - le - lu - - ia.

5. Riu, riu, chiu

Words of unknown authorship

ascribed to
MATEO FLECHA the elder (1481–1553)

[Vivace]
TENOR or BASS SOLO
Ri - u, ri - u, chi - u La___ guar-da ri - be - ra:
Dios guar - do el lo - bo De___ nues - tra cor - de - ra,
Dios guar - do el lo - bo De___ nues - tra cor - de - ra.
REFRAIN (full choir)
S.
A.
T.
B.
Ri - u, ri - u, chi - u, La___ guar - da ri - be - ra:
Dios guar - do el
Dios guar -
Dios guar - do el lo - bo
- do el lo - bo, el lo - bo
De___ nues - tra cor - de - ra,
lo - bo, el lo - bo
Dios guar - do el lo - bo
FINE
Dios guar - do el lo - bo, el lo - bo
De___ nues - tra cor - de - ra.
Dios guar - do el lo - bo, el lo - bo

VERSE 1
27
SOLO
1. El lo - bo ra - bio - so La___ qui - so mor - der, Mas Dios po - de - ro - so La su-po de-fen - der;
35
REFRAIN D.S.
Qui - so - le ha - zer que No pu - die - sse pe - car, Ni aun o - ri - gi - nal Es - ta Vir - gen no tu - vie - ra.
43
VERSE 2
2. Es - te ques na - çi - do Es___ el gran Mo - nar - cha, Chri - sto pa - tri - ar - ca De___ car - ne ves - ti - do;
51
REFRAIN D.S.
Ha nos re - di - mi - do Con se ha - zer chi - qui - to: Aun - que e - ra in - fi - ni - to Fi - ni - to se hi - zie - ra.
59
VERSE 3
3. Mu - chas pro - fe - ci - as Lo han pro - fe - ti - za - do; Y aun en nues - tros di - as Lo he - mos al - can - ça - do.
67
REFRAIN D.S.
A Dios hu - ma - na - do Ve - mos en el sue - lo Y al hom - bre en el cie - lo Por - que él le qui - sie - ra.
75
VERSE 4
4. Pues que ya te - ne - mos Lo___ que de - se - a - mos, To - dos jun - tos va - mos, Pre - sen - tes lle - ve - mos;
83
REFRAIN D.S.
To - dos le da - re - mos Nues - tra vo - lun - tad, Pues a se i - gua - lar Con el___ hom - bre vi - nie - ra.

Translation of text:

Refrain: 'Riu, riu, chiu' cried the shepherd by the riverside. God kept the wolf [Satan] away from our lamb [the Virgin Mary].

1. The raging wolf wanted to bite her, but the more powerful God knew how to protect her. He wanted to make her incapable of sin, and this Virgin did not even have original sin [because of her immaculate conception].

2. He who is born is a great King, Christ the Patriarch clothed in human flesh. He has redeemed us by making himself a child: although he is immortal, he made himself mortal.

3. Many prophecies have foretold it; and in our time we have seen it fulfilled. We see God in human form here on earth, and man raised to heaven because God loved him.

4. Since now we have our hearts' desire, let us all go together bearing gifts; we shall all submit our will to him, because he came to make himself equal with man.

6. Resonet in laudibus

(Let the voice of praise resound)

Words: 14th-century German
English version by John Rutter

JACOB HANDL (Gallus)
(1550–91)

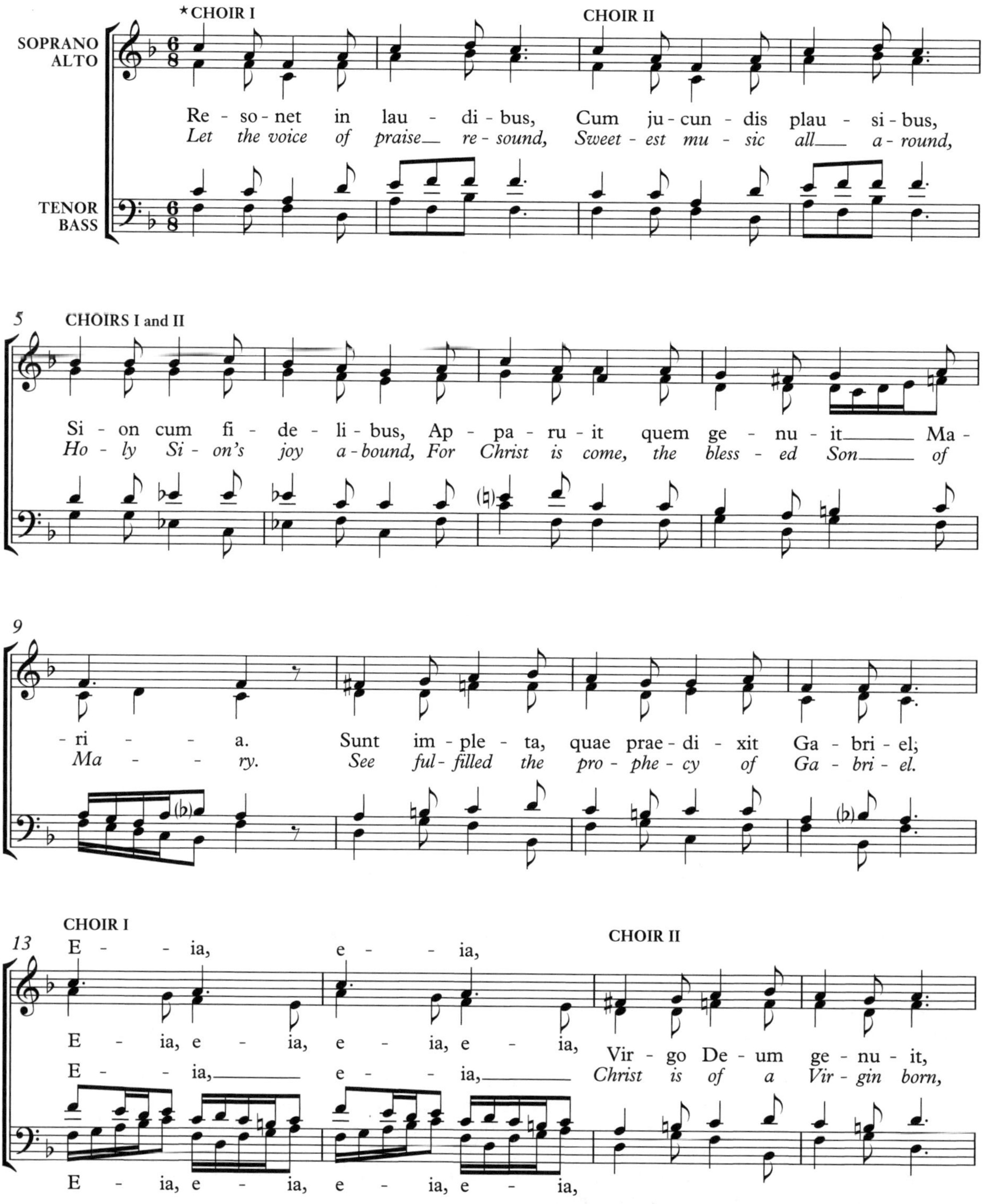

* The Choir I–Choir II indications are Handl's own, but the whole setting may be sung by full choir.

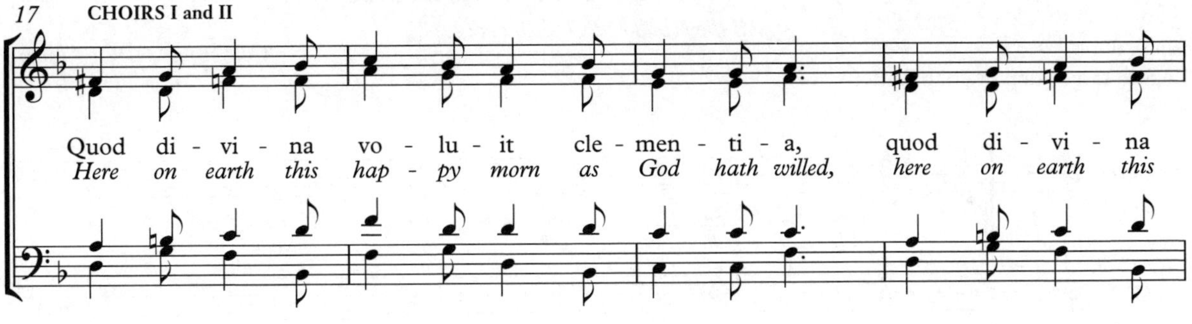
17
CHOIRS I and II
Quod di - vi - na vo - lu - it cle - men - ti - a, quod di - vi - na
Here on earth this hap - py morn as God hath willed, here on earth this

21
CHOIR I
vo - lu - it cle - men - ti - a. Ho - di - e ap - pa - ru - it, ap -
hap - py morn as God hath willed. On this day in Beth - le - hem, in

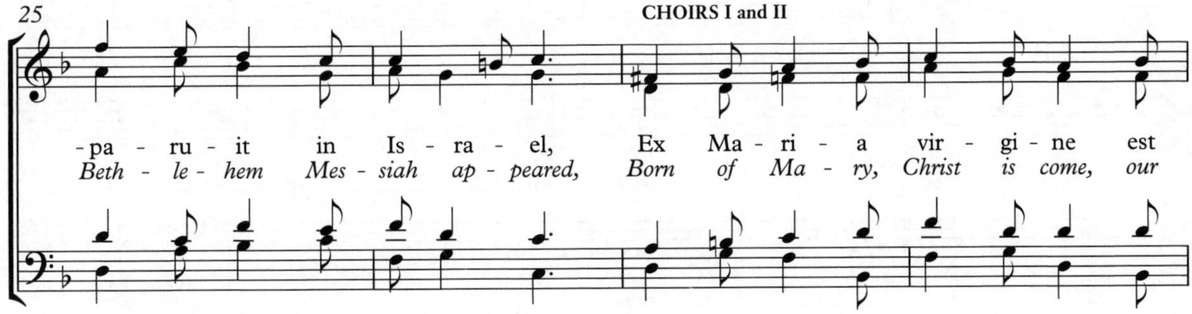
25
CHOIRS I and II
-pa - ru - it in Is - ra - el, Ex Ma - ri - a vir - gi - ne est
Beth - le - hem Mes - siah ap - peared, Born of Ma - ry, Christ is come, our

29
*
na - tus Rex, ex Ma - ri - a vir - gi - ne est na - tus Rex.
Lord and King, born of Ma - ry, Christ is come, our Lord and King.

* The rests in the alto, tenor, and bass voices are 'figleaves' to avoid parallel octaves and fifths with the next chord. Conductors wishing to observe them should probably also insert them in bar 19 (where they are absent in the source). Alternatively, it may be better for all four voices in bar 29 to sing 'Rex' as a crotchet (quarter note).

7. Omnes de Saba venient

(*All they shall out of Sheba come*)

Isaiah 60: 6
English translation by John Rutter

JACOB HANDL (Gallus)
(1550–91)

11
S.
au - - rum et thus de - -
bring - - ing gold and in - -
A.
- - ba ve - - - ni - ent, au - - rum et thus de -
of She - - - ba come, bring - - ing gold and in -
T.
- ba ve - - - - - ni - ent, au - rum et thus de -
of She - - - - - ba come, bring - ing gold and in -
- ent, de Sa - ba ve - - ni - ent, au - rum et thus de - fe - ren -
come, shall out of She - - ba come, bring - ing gold and in - cense with
B.
ve - - ni - ent, au - - rum et thus de -
She - - ba come, bring - - ing gold and in -
p
16
S.
- fe - ren - - tes, au - - - rum et thus de - fe - ren -
- cense with them, bring - - ing gold and in - cense with
A.
- fe - ren - tes, au - rum et thus de - fe - ren - tes, et
- cense with them, bring - ing gold and in - cense with them, and
T.
- fe - ren - tes, au - rum et thus de - fe - ren - tes,
- cense with them, bring - ing gold and in - cense with them,
- tes, au - rum et thus de - fe - ren - tes, de - fe - ren -
them, bring - ing gold and in - cense with them, in - cense with
B.
- fe - ren - tes, au - - - rum et thus de - fe - ren -
- cense with them, bring - - ing gold and in - cense with
mp

21
S.
-tes, et lau - - - - - - dem Do - mi - no an - nun - ti -
them, and prais - - - - - - ing God the Lord, his glo - ry
A.
lau - - - dem Do - - - mi - no an - nun - ti - an - tes,
prais - - - ing God the Lord, his glo - ry tell - ing,
T.
et lau - - - dem Do - mi - no an - nun - - -
and prais - - - ing God the Lord, his glo - - -
-tes, et lau - - - dem Do - mi - no an - nun - ti -
them, and prais - - - ing God the Lord, his glo - ry
B.
-tes,
them,
f
f
26
S.
- an - - - - tes, et lau - - - dem
tell - - - - ing, and prais - - - ing
A.
an - nun - ti - an - - tes, et lau -
his glo - ry tell - - ing, and prais -
T.
- ti - an - - tes, et lau - - - dem Do - mi -
- ry tell - - ing, and prais - - - ing God the
-an - - tes, et lau - - - dem Do - mi - no,
tell - - ing, and prais - - - ing God the Lord,
B.
et lau - - - dem Do - mi - no an - -
and prais - - - ing God the Lord, his

30
S.
Do - mi - no, et lau - - - dem, et lau - - - -
God the Lord, and prais - - - ing, and prais - - - -
A.
- - dem Do - - mi - no an - nun - ti - an - - tes, et
- - ing God the Lord, his glo - ry tell - - ing, and
T.
- no, et lau - - - dem Do - mi - no, et lau - -
Lord, and prais - - - - ing God the Lord, and prais -
et lau - - - - dem, et lau - - - - - dem
and prais - - - - ing, and prais - - - - - ing
B.
- nun - ti - an - - tes, et lau - - - - dem Do - mi -
glo - ry tell - - ing, and prais - - - - ing God the
34
S.
- dem Do - mi - no an - nun - ti - an - - - - tes.
- ing God the Lord, his glo - ry tell - - - - ing.
A.
lau - - - dem Do - mi - no an - nun - ti - an - tes.
prais - - - ing God the Lord, his glo - ry tell - ing.
T.
- - dem Do - mi - no an - nun - - ti - an - tes.
- - ing God the Lord, his glo - - ry tell - ing.
Do - mi - no an - nun - - - - - ti - an - tes. Al - le - -
God the Lord, his glo - - - - - ry tell - ing.
B.
- no an - nun - - - ti - an - - - - tes. Al -
Lord, his glo - - - ry tell - - - - ing.

38
S. Al - le - - - - - - - lu - ia, al - le -
A. Al - le - - - lu - ia,
T. Al - le - - - lu - - - ia, al -
- lu - ia, al - le - - lu - ia, al - le - - lu - ia,
B. - le - - lu - ia, al - le - - lu - ia, al - le - - lu -
43
S. - - - - - - - - lu - ia.
A. al - le - - - - lu - ia, al - le - - - - lu - ia.
T. -le - - - - - - lu - - ia, al - le - - - - - lu - ia.
al - le - - lu - ia.
B. -ia, al - le - - lu - ia, al - le - - - - - lu - ia.

8. Frohlocket, ihr Völker auf Erden

(Rejoice and be glad, all ye people)

Words: Sentence for Christmastide*
English translation by John Rutter

F. MENDELSSOHN (1809–47)
Op. 79 no. 1

* See editorial commentary (p. 123).

5
[mf]
S.
Der Hei-land ist er - schie - nen, ist er - schie - nen, den der Herr ver -
The Sa-viour now ap - pear - eth, now ap - pear - eth, whom the Lord hath
Hei - land ist er - schie - nen, der Hei-land ist er - schie - nen, den der Herr ver -
Sa - viour now ap - pear - eth, the Sa-viour now ap - pear - eth, whom the Lord hath
A.
ist er - schie - nen, der Hei-land ist er - schie - nen, den der Herr ver -
now ap - pear - eth, the Sa-viour now ap - pear - eth, whom the Lord hath
ist er - schie - nen, der Hei-land ist er - schie - nen, den der Herr ver -
now ap - pear - eth, the Sa-viour now ap - pear - eth, whom the Lord hath
T.
[mf]
-lock - et, ihr Völ - ker auf Er - den! Der Hei-land ist er - schie - nen, den der Herr ver -
-joice and be glad, all ye peo - ple! The Sa-viour now ap - pear - eth, whom the Lord hath
[mf]
-lock - et, ihr Völ - ker auf Er - den! Der Hei-land ist er - schie - nen, den der Herr ver -
-joice and be glad, all ye peo - ple! The Sa-viour now ap - pear - eth, whom the Lord hath
B.
[mf]
-lock - et, ihr Völ - ker auf Er - den! Der Hei-land ist er - schie - nen, den der Herr ver -
-joice and be glad, all ye peo - ple! The Sa-viour now ap - pear - eth, whom the Lord hath
[mf]
-lock - et, ihr Völ - ker auf Er - den! Der Hei-land ist er - schie - nen, den der Herr ver -
-joice and be glad, all ye peo - ple! The Sa-viour now ap - pear - eth, whom the Lord hath
mf

10
f
[mf]
S.
A.
T.
B.
-heis - sen. Er hat sei - ne Ge - rech - tig - keit der Welt of - fen - ba - - ret. Hal - le -
pro - mised. Lo! his glo - ry and right - eous - ness shine forth to all na - - tions.
-heis - sen. Er hat sei - ne Ge - rech - tig - keit der Welt of - fen - ba - - - ret.
pro - mised. Lo! his glo - ry and right - eous - ness shine forth to all na - - - tions.
mf

16
S.
A.
T.
B.
f
[mf]
- lu - ja, Hal - le - lu - ja! Er hat sei - ne Ge - rech - tig - keit der Welt of - fen -
Lo! his glo - ry and right - eous-ness shine forth to all
Hal - le - lu - ja! Er hat sei - ne Ge - rech - tig - keit der Welt of - fen -
Lo! his glo - ry and right - eous-ness shine forth to all
- lu - ja, Hal - le - lu - ja! Er hat sei - ne Ge - rech - tig - keit der Welt of - fen -
Lo! his glo - ry and right - eous-ness shine forth to all
Hal - le - lu - - - ja! Er hat sei - ne Ge - rech - tig - keit der Welt of - fen -
Lo! his glo - ry and right - eous-ness shine forth to all
- lu - ja, Hal - le - lu - ja! Er hat sei - ne Ge - rech - tig - keit der Welt of - fen -
Lo! his glo - ry and right - eous-ness shine forth to all
Hal - le - lu - ja, Hal - le - lu - ja! Er hat sei - ne Ge - rech - tig - keit der Welt of - fen -
Lo! his glo - ry and right - eous-ness shine forth to all
- lu - - ja, Hal - le - lu - ja! Er hat sei - ne Ge - rech - tig - keit der Welt of - fen -
Lo! his glo - ry and right - eous-ness shine forth to all
Hal - le - lu - ja! Er hat sei - ne Ge - rech - tig - keit der Welt of - fen -
Lo! his glo - ry and right - eous-ness shine forth to all

22
[mf]
- ba - ret. Hal - le - lu - ja, Hal - le - lu - ja, Hal - le - lu - ja, Hal - le -
na - tions.
S.
[mf]
- ba - - ret. Hal - le - lu - ja, Hal - le - lu -
na - - tions.
[mf]
- ba - ret. Hal - le - lu - ja, Hal - le - lu - - ja, Hal - le - lu - ja,
na - tions.
A.
[mf]
- ba - ret. Hal - le - lu - ja, Hal - le - lu - - ja, Hal -
na - tions.
[mf]
- ba - ret. Hal - le - lu - ja, Hal - le - lu - - ja, Hal - le - lu - ja,
na - tions.
T.
[mf]
- ba - - ret. Hal - le - lu - ja, Hal - le - lu - - ja, Hal - le -
na - - tions.
[mf]
- ba - ret. Hal - le - lu - ja, Hal - le - lu - ja, Hal - le - lu - ja,
na - tions.
B.
[mf]
- ba - - ret. Hal - le - lu - - ja, Hal - le - lu - -
na - - tions.
mf

28
S.
- lu - ja, Hal - le - lu - ja! Froh - lock - et, ihr Völ - ker auf Er - den. Hal-le - lu - - ja!
Re - joice and be glad, all ye peo - ple.
- ja, Hal - le - lu - ja! Froh - lock - et, ihr Völ - ker auf Er - den. Hal-le - lu - - ja!
Re - joice and be glad, all ye peo - ple.
A.
Hal - le - lu - ja! Froh - lock - et, ihr Völ - ker auf Er - den. Hal-le - lu - ja!
Re - joice and be glad, all ye peo - ple.
- - le - lu - ja! Froh - lock - et, ihr Völ - ker auf Er - den. Hal-le - lu - - ja!
Re - joice and be glad, all ye peo - ple.
T.
Hal - le - lu - ja, Hal - le - lu - - ja!
- lu - ja, Hal - le - lu - - ja, Hal - le - lu - - ja!
B.
Hal - le - lu - - - - - ja, Hal - le - lu - - ja!
- ja, Hal - le - lu - - ja, Hal - le - lu - - ja!
f

9. Nesciens mater

Antiphon for the Octave of the Nativity

JEAN MOUTON
(1459–1522)

A mother knowing no man

3
S.
ma - - ter, ne - - sci - ens ma - ter vir -
ma - ter vir - - - - go
A.
ma - - ter vir - - go vi - - - rum,
ne - - sci - ens ma - ter vir - go vi - - - rum
T.
vir - - - go vi - rum pe - pe - rit
ma - - ter vir - go vi -
B.
vir - - go vi - - rum,
vir - go vi - - rum
cresc.
mp
a virgin,
brought forth
6
S.
-go vi - - - rum pe - pe - - rit, pe - pe - rit
vi - rum pe - pe - rit si - ne do - lo - re, si - ne do -
A.
vi - rum pe - pe -
pe - pe - - rit, pe - - pe - rit
T.
si - ne do - lo - re, si - ne do - - lo - re,
- rum pe - pe - - - - -
B.
vi - rum pe - pe - rit
pe - pe - - - - rit si -
dim.
p
without pain . . .

9
S.
si - - ne do - lo - re Sal - va - - -
-lo - re, do - - - lo - re
A.
-rit si - - ne do - lo - - -
si - - ne do - lo - re Sal - va - - to - - - rem
T.
do - - - lo - re
-rit si - ne do - lo - - re, pe - - pe - rit
B.
si - - ne do - lo - - - re
-ne do - lo - re, pe - - pe - rit si - - ne do - lo -
cresc.
mp
. . . the eternal Saviour;
12
S.
- to - - rem sae - - cu - lo - - - rum, Sal -
Sal - va - - to - rem,
A.
- re Sal - - va - to - - - rem
sae - - cu - lo - - rum, Sal - va - to - - - - rem
T.
Sal - va - - to - rem, Sal - - va - to -
si - - ne do - lo - re Sal - - va - to - - - rem
B.
Sal - - va - to - - rem sae- - - - - -
- re Sal - - va - to - - rem sae - cu - lo -
cresc.
mf

15
S.
-va - to - - - - rem sae - cu - lo - rum ip - sum Re -
Sal - - va - to - rem sae - cu -
A.
sae - - - - - - - cu - lo - rum
sae - cu - lo - rum ip - sum Re - gem, ip - sum Re - gem
T.
- rem sae - cu - lo - rum ip - sum Re -
sae - cu - lo - - rum ip -
B.
- cu - lo - rum ip - sum Re - gem
- rum ip - - sum Re - gem,
dim.
p
and this same King of angels . . .
18
S.
-gem, ip - sum Re - gem An - - ge - lo - - - - - -
- lo - rum ip - sum Re - - - gem An - - - ge -
A.
ip - sum Re - gem
An - - ge - lo - - - - - - rum
T.
- - - gem An - - ge - lo - rum
- - sum Re - gem, ip - - sum Re -
B.
An - ge - lo - - -
ip - - sum Re - gem An - - ge - lo -

21
S.
A.
T.
B.
-rum so - la vir - go, so - la vir -
- lo - rum so - la vir - go,
An - ge - lo - rum
so - la vir - go, so - la vir - go,
so - la vir - go, so - la
- gem An - ge - lo - rum so - la vir - go,
- rum
- rum so - la vir - go, so - la
cresc.
. . . did she, alone a virgin [mother],
24
S.
A.
T.
B.
go, so - la vir - go, so - la vir - go
so - la vir - go, so - la vir - go
so - la vir - go
so - la vir - go, so - la vir - go la - cta -
vir - go, so - la vir - go la - cta - bat,
so - la vir - go, so - la vir - go la - cta -
so - la vir - go la - cta -
vir - go, so - la vir - go la - cta - bat,
mp
cresc.
mf
suckle . . .

. . . at her breast, filled [with milk] from heaven.

31
S.
-bat u - be - ra de cae - lo, de cae - - lo
so - la vir - go la - cta - - bat u - be - ra de
A.
- - cta - bat u - - be - ra
de cae - lo, de cae - lo ple - na, de
T.
- - bat u - be - ra de cae - lo, de cae -
u - - be - ra de cae - lo ple - na, u -
B.
u - be - ra de cae - - -
de cae - lo ple - na, u - - be - ra de
cresc.
f dolce
34
ple - na, de cae - lo ple - na, u -
cae - lo, de cae - lo ple - na, so - la vir -
- de cae - - - lo ple - na, u - be -
cae - lo ple - na, u - be - ra de cae -
- lo ple - na, so - la vir - go la - cta - - bat
- be - ra de cae - lo ple - na, u -
- lo ple - - na, u - - be - ra de cae - lo,
cae - lo ple - na, u - - be - ra de cae -
dim.
mp
cresc.

37
S.
- be - ra de cae - lo, de cae - - lo ple - na,
-go la - cta - - bat u - be - ra de cae - lo,
A.
-ra de cae - lo, u - be - ra de
-lo, de cae - lo ple - na, de cae - lo ple -
T.
u - be - ra de cae - lo, de cae - lo ple -
- be - ra de cae - lo ple - na, u - - be - ra
B.
- lo ple -
- lo ple - na, u - be - ra de cae - lo ple -
mf
40
de cae - lo ple - - na.
de cae - lo ple - - na.
cae - - - - lo ple - - - - na.
-na, de cae - lo ple - - - - na.
- na, ple - - - - na.
de cae - lo ple - - na.
-na, de cae - lo ple - - na.
-na, de cae - lo ple - - na.
dim.

10. Hodie Christus natus est

Antiphon at Christmas Day Vespers

G. P. da PALESTRINA
(1525–94)

Today Christ was born: *Nowell, Nowell:*

Today the Saviour appeared:

Today on earth . . .

32
S.1
- - - - nunt an - - ge - li, lae - tan - - - - - -
S.2
- - nunt an - - ge - li, lae - tan - - - - - tur arch -
A.1
ca - - nunt an - - ge - li, lae - tan - - tur
B.1
- nunt an - - - ge - li, lae -
A.2
ca - - - nunt an - ge - li,
T.1
- ra ca - - - nunt an - ge - li,
T.2
ca - - - nunt an - ge - li,
B.2
ca - - nunt an - - - ge - li,
dim.
mf
the angels sing,
the archangels rejoice:
37
S.1
- - tur arch - an - - - ge - li: no - e, no-
S.2
- an - - - - - - - - - ge - li: no - e, no-
A.1
arch - - an - - - - ge - li: no - e, no-
B.1
- tan - - tur arch - an - - ge - li: no - e, no-
A.2
no - e, no - e, no - e:
T.1
no - e, no - e, no - e:
T.2
no - e, no - e, no - e:
B.2
no - e, no - e, no - e:

42
S.1
- e, no - e.
S.2
- e, no - e.
A.1
- e, no - e.
B.1
- e, no - e.
A.2
Ho - di - e ex - sul - - tant ju - sti,
T.1
Ho - di - e ex - sul - - - tant ju - sti, di - cen - -
T.2
Ho - di - e ex - sul - - - - tant ju - - - sti, di -
B.2
Ho - di - e ex - sul - - - tant ju - sti, di - -
Today the righteous exult, saying:
47
S.1
Glo - - ri - a in ex - cel - - - - - - sis
S.2
Glo - - ri - a in ex - cel - - - - - sis
A.1
Glo - - ri - a in ex - - cel - - sis
B.1
Glo - - ri - a in ex - - cel - - sis
A.2
di - cen - - tes:
T.1
- tes:
T.2
- - - cen - tes:
B.2
- - cen - tes:
dim.
p
cresc.
Glory to God in the highest.

52
S.1 De - o, glo - ri - a in ex -
S.2 De - - - o, glo - - ri - a in ex -
A.1 De - - - - o, glo - ri - a in
B.1 De - - - - o, glo - - - ri - a in
A.2 Glo - - ri - a, glo - - ri - a in ex -
T.1 Glo - - ri - a, glo - ri - a in ex -
T.2 Glo - - ri - a, glo - - - ri - a in ex -
B.2 Glo - - ri - a, glo - - - ri - a in ex -
mf
cresc.
f
57
S.1 - cel - sis De - - - - - - - - o, De - - - o:
S.2 - cel - sis De - - - - - - - - - - o:
A.1 ex - cel - - - sis De - - - - - - - o:
B.1 ex - - - - cel - - sis De - - - - - - - - o:
A.2 - cel - - - - sis De - - - - - - - - o: no -
T.1 - cel - sis De - - - - o, De - - - o: no -
T.2 - cel - sis De - - - o, in ex - cel - sis De - - o: no -
B.2 - cel - - - - sis De - - - - - o: no -
[♩. = 𝅗𝅥 of preceding]
mf

* Conductors may wish to shorten these notes to two beats' length, to match the 2nd alto.

11. O beatum et sacrosanctum diem

(O how blest is the day)

Antiphon for Christmas Day
English translation by John Rutter

PETER PHILIPS
(1561–1628)

9
S.
-a pro no - - bis na - sci di - gna - tus est.
-ing, for us was born of a Vir - gin mild.
-a pro no - - - - - - bis na - sci di - gna - tus est.
-ing, for us was born of a Vir - gin mild.
A.
-a pro no - - - - bis na - sci di - gna - tus est.
-ing, for us was born of a Vir - gin mild.
T.
-a pro no - - - - - bis na - sci di - gna - tus est.
-ing, for us was born of a Vir - gin mild.
B.
13
S.
Gau - de - at i - ta - que u - ni - ver - sus or - bis,
Glo - ri - a! glo - ri - a! let the whole earth praise him,
Gau - de - at i - ta - que u - ni - ver - sus or - bis, gau - de - at,
Glo - ri - a! glo - ri - a! let the whole earth praise him, glo - ri - a!
A.
Gau - de - at i - ta - que u - ni - ver - sus or - bis, gau - de - at,
Glo - ri - a! glo - ri - a! let the whole earth praise him, glo - ri - a!
T.
Gau - de - at i - ta - que u - ni - ver - sus or - bis, gau - de - at,
Glo - ri - a! glo - ri - a! let the whole earth praise him, glo - ri - a!
B.
Gau - de - at i - ta - que u - ni - ver - sus or - bis, gau - de - at,
Glo - ri - a! glo - ri - a! let the whole earth praise him, glo - ri - a!
Vivace (♩. = ♩ of preceding = 50)
f marc.

19
S.
gau - de - at i - ta - que u - ni - ver - sus or - -
glo - ri - a! glo - ri - a! let the whole earth praise
gau - de - at i - ta - que u - ni - ver - sus or - - - -
glo - ri - a! glo - ri - a! let the whole earth praise
A.
gau - de - at i - ta - que u - ni - ver - sus or - - - -
glo - ri - a! glo - ri - a! let the whole earth praise
T.
gau - de - at i - ta - que u - ni - ver - sus or - -
glo - ri - a! glo - ri - a! let the whole earth praise
B.
gau - de - at i - ta - que u - ni - ver - sus or - -
glo - ri - a! glo - ri - a! let the whole earth praise
24
S.
-bis, et can - te - mus il - li in so - no tu -
him, sing - ing and re - joic - ing with sound of trum -
-bis, et can - te - mus il - li, et can - te - mus il - li in so - no
him, sing - ing and re - joic - ing, sing - ing and re - joic - ing with sound of
A.
-bis, et can - te - mus il - li, et can - te - mus il - li in
him, sing - ing and re - joic - ing, sing - ing and re - joic - ing with
T.
-bis, et can - te - mus il - li, et can - te - mus il - li in so - no
him, sing - ing and re - joic - ing, sing - ing and re - joic - ing with sound of
B.
-bis, et can - te - mus il - li in
him, sing - ing and re - joic - ing with
Tempo I
mf grazioso
marcato

27
S.
- bae, in so - no tu - - bae, in so - no tu - - bae, in so - no
- pet, with sound of trum - pet, with sound of trum - pet, with sound of
tu - bae, in so - no tu - bae, in so - no tu - bae, in
trum - pet, with sound of trum - pet, with sound of trum - pet, with
A.
so - no tu - bae, in so - no tu - - bae, in so - no tu -
sound of trum - pet, with sound of trum - pet, with sound of trum -
T.
tu - bae, in so - no tu - bae, in so - no tu - bae, in
trum - pet, with sound of trum - pet, with sound of trum - pet, with
B.
so - - - no tu - - - - - - -
sound of trum - - - - - - -
cresc.
29
S.
tu - bae, in so - no tu - bae, in so - no tu - bae, in
trum - pet, with sound of trum - pet, with sound of trum - pet, with
so - no tu - bae, in so - no tu - bae, in so - no tu -
sound of trum - pet, with sound of trum - pet, with sound of trum -
A.
- bae, in so - no tu - bae, in so - no tu - bae, in so - no
- pet, with sound of trum - pet, with sound of trum - pet, with sound of
T.
so - no tu - bae, in so - no tu - bae, in so - no tu -
sound of trum - pet, with sound of trum - pet, with sound of trum -
B.
- bae, in so - - no tu - - -
- pet, with sound of trum - - -
f

31
S.
so - no tu - - bae, ci - - - - tha - ra, psal - te - ri-
sound of trum - pet, mer - - - - ry harp, with string and
-bae, in so - no tu - bae, ci - - - - tha - ra, psal - te - ri - o
-pet, with sound of trum - pet, mer - - - - ry harp, with string and pipe,
A.
tu - - - - bae, psal - te - ri - o et or - ga-
trum - - - - pet, with string and pipe, with string and
T.
-bae, in so - no tu - bae, ci - - - - tha - ra, psal - te - ri - o et or - ga-
-pet, with sound of trum - pet, mer - - - - ry harp, with string and pipe, with string and
B.
- - - - bae, psal - te - ri - o et or - ga-
- - - - pet, with string and pipe, with string and
dim.
mf leggiero
34
S.
-o et or - ga - no, psal - te - ri - o et or - ga - no. Con - gra - tu -
pipe, with string and pipe, with string and pipe, with string and pipe. Give thanks un -
et or - ga - no, psal - te - ri - o et or - ga - no. Con - gra - tu -
with string and pipe, with string and pipe, with string and pipe. Give thanks un -
A.
-no, psal - te - ri - o et or - ga - no. Con - gra - tu - le -
pipe, with string and pipe, with string and pipe. Give thanks un - to
T.
-no, psal - te - ri - o et or - ga - no. Con - gra - tu -
pipe, with string and pipe, with string and pipe. Give thanks un -
B.
-no, psal - te - ri - o et or - ga - no. Con - gra - tu -
pipe, with string and pipe, with string and pipe. Give thanks un -
f

37
S.
A.
T.
B.
- le - - mur
- to him
- le - - mur cum mul - ti - tu - di - ne an - ge - lo - - rum ex - er - ci -
- to him with all the host of hea - ven u - ni - - ting in joy - ful
- - mur cum mul - ti - tu - di - ne an - ge - lo - - rum ex - er - ci -
him with all the host of hea - ven u - ni - - ting in joy - ful
- le - - mur cum mul - ti - tu - di - ne an - ge - lo - rum ex - er - ci -
- to him with all the host of hea - ven u - ni - ting in joy - ful
- le - - mur cum mul - ti - tu - di - ne an - ge - lo - - rum ex - er - ci -
- to him with all the host of hea - ven u - ni - - ting in joy - ful
mf
40
ex - er - ci - tus, ex - er - ci - tus, sem - per su - as lau - - -
in joy - ful song, in joy - ful song, sing - ing prais - es, prais - -
- tus, ex - er - ci - tus, sem - per su - as lau - -
song, in joy - ful song, sing - ing prais - es, prais - -
- tus, ex - er - ci - tus, sem - - per su - - as lau -
song, in joy - ful song, sing - - ing prais - - es, prais -
- tus, ex - er - ci - tus, sem - per su - as lau - - -
song, in joy - ful song, sing - ing prais - es, prais - - -
- tus, ex - er - ci - tus, sem - - per su - as lau -
song, in joy - ful song, sing - - ing prais - es, prais -
f

* 'Alleluia' is given as an alternative to 'Noë' in the original edition of 1612.

51
S.
- ë, no - ë, no - ë, no - ë, no - ë, no - ë, no -
- well, no - well, no - well, no - well, no - well, no - well, no - well, no -
- ë, no - ë, no - ë, no - ë, no - ë, no - ë, no - ë, no -
- well, no - well, no - well, no - well, no - well, no - well, no - well, no -
A.
- ë, no - ë, no - ë, no - ë, no - ë, no - ë, no - ë, no - ë, no - ë, no - ë, no - ë, no -
- well, no - well, no - well, no - well, no - well, no - well, no - well, no - well, no - well, no - well, no - well, no -
T.
- ë, no - ë, no - ë, no - ë, no - ë, no - ë, no - ë, no - ë, no - ë, no - ë, no - ë, no -
- well, no - well, no - well, no - well, no - well, no - well, no - well, no - well, no - well, no - well, no - well, no -
B.
no - ë, no - ë, no - ë, no - ë, no - ë, no - ë, no -
no - well, no - well, no - well, no - well, no - well, no - well, no -
cresc.
mf
cresc.
f
54
S.
- ë, no - ë, no - ë, no - ë, no - ë, no - ë, no - ë, no - ë.
- well, no - well, no - well, no - well, no - well, no - well, no - well, no - well.
- ë, no - ë, no - ë, no - ë, no - ë, no - ë, no - ë, no - ë.
- well, no - well, no - well, no - well, no - well, no - well, no - well, no - well.
A.
- ë, no - ë, no - ë, no - ë, no - ë, no - ë, no - ë, no - ë, no - ë, no - ë, no - ë, no - ë.
- well, no - well, no - well, no - well, no - well, no - well, no - well, no - well, no - well, no - well, no - well, no - well.
T.
- ë, no - ë, no - ë, no - ë, no - ë, no - ë, no - ë, no - ë.
- well, no - well, no - well, no - well, no - well, no - well, no - well, no - well.
B.
- ë, no - ë, no - ë, no - ë, no - ë, no - ë, no - ë, no - ë.
- well, no - well, no - well, no - well, no - well, no - well, no - well, no - well.

12. In dulci jubilo

Words: German traditional

Old German carol
Setting by HIERONYMUS PRAETORIUS
(1560–1629)

1. In a sweet hymn of praise — *now sing and rejoice!*
3. O the goodness of the Father, — *O the gentleness of the Son!*

* The apparently illogical rests here and in bars 4, 12, 17, 20, and 28 are 'figleaves' to avoid parallel unisons, fifths or octaves.

† The organ part is editorial and optional.

* See footnote on p. 78.

8
S.1
-o, Und leuch-tet als die Son - ne Ma-tris in gre - mi -
-na, So hat er uns er - wor - ben Cae - lo - rum gau - di -
S.2
-o, Und leuch-tet als die Son - ne Ma-tris in gre - mi -
-na, So hat er uns er - wor - ben Cae - lo - rum gau - di -
A.1
-o, Und leuch-tet als die Son - ne Ma-tris in gre - mi-o,
-na, So hat er uns er - wor - ben Cae - lo - rum gau - di-a,
T.1
- - pi-o, Und leuch-tet als die Son - ne Ma-tris in gre - -
- - mi-na, So hat er uns er - wor - ben Cae - lo - rum gau - -
A.2
- pi - o, Und leuch-tet als die Son - - ne Ma-tris in gre - -
- mi - na, So hat er uns er - wor - - ben Cae - lo - rum gau - -
T.2
- - pi-o, Und leuch-tet als die Son - ne Ma-tris in gre - -
- - mi-na, So hat er uns er - wor - ben Cae - lo - rum gau - -
B.1
-o, Und leuch-tet als die Son - ne Ma-tris in gre - mi -
-na, So hat er uns er - wor - ben Cae - lo - rum gau - di -
B.2
-o, Und leuch-tet als die Son - ne Ma-tris in gre - mi -
-na, So hat er uns er - wor - ben Cae - lo - rum gau - di -
And shines like the sun
But he has gained for us
in his mother's lap.
the joys of heaven.

You are Alpha and Omega.
O that we were there!

* See footnote on p. 78.

2. O Jesu, little one,
4. Where are those joys?

I yearn for you so much!
Nowhere but there!

Comfort my spirit,
There the angels are singing

O supreme Child,
new songs

Through all your goodness,
And there the bells are ringing

O Prince of glory,
In the court of the King.

Make me follow you.
O that we were there!

13. Quem pastores laudavere

Words: 14th-century German

MICHAEL PRAETORIUS
(?1571–1621)

The section for four solo sopranos may alternatively be sung by full sopranos. The organ accompaniment is optional (see editorial notes) but if it is used here it should continue throughout the choral section, doubling the voice parts.

Translation of text:

1. [Glory to Christ] whom the shepherds praised, the shepherds to whom the angel said 'Be not afraid, the King of glory is born'. Now the glory of the angels has shone forth to men on earth; the Virgin Mother has newly given birth and brought joy, and the true sun has lightened the darkness. Christ is born today of a Virgin: a King is born without earthly father.

2. [Glory to Christ] to whom the wise men came, bringing gold, frankincense and myrrh; they offered these gifts with true heart to the Lion of Judah [*lit.* lion of victory]. Today remission of our sins is granted: let guilty mankind rejoice. Light has shone from heaven, peace has now been restored, she who bore the Saviour has remained sinless. Christ is born today of a Virgin: a King is born without earthly father.

3. To Christ the King, Son of God, given to us through Mary, let praise, honour and glory worthily and truly resound. The great name of the Lord is Emmanuel, which means, God with us. Let us rejoice in the salvation of the Redeemer Lord; this is the day and the year of rejoicing. Children, raise your voices together and make music, sing with reverent voice and clap your hands.

Note: The Latin text of the first sentence of each verse makes grammatical sense only when verse 3 is reached.

14. In dulci jubilo

Words: German traditional
English version by R. L. Pearsall (1795–1856)

SAMUEL SCHEIDT
(1587–1654)

* The trumpet parts are denoted by the composer as optional.

† The organ part is editorial and optional. Exceptionally, editorial dynamic markings are shown in the voice parts.

7
S. 1
- ci ju - bi - lo, in dul - ci ju - bi - lo, ju - - - bi -
S. 2
- - bi - lo, in dul - ci ju - bi - lo, in dul - ci ju - - bi -
A. 1
in dul - ci ju - bi - lo, in dul - ci ju - - - - - bi -
f dolce
T. 1
In dul - ci ju - bi - lo, in dul - ci ju - bi - lo.
A. 2
T. 2
B. 1
B. 2
Tpts

13
S. 1
- lo.
S. 2
- lo.
A. 1
- lo.
T. 1
A. 2
f
In dul- ci ju - bi - lo, ju-bi - lo, in dul - ci ju - bi - lo, in
T. 2
f
In dul - ci ju - bi - lo, in dul - ci ju - bi - lo, in dul - ci
B. 1
f
In dul - ci ju - - - - bi - lo, in
B. 2
f
In dul - ci ju - bi - lo, in dul - ci ju - bi - lo,
Tpts

* Original time signature ¢ 3/2 . Note values halved in this and the other triple-time sections.

26
S. 1
Nun sing - et und seid froh!
Let us our hom - age shew,
S. 2
Nun sing - et und seid froh!
Let us our hom - age shew,
A. 1
Nun sing - et und seid froh!
Let us our hom - age shew,
T. 1
Nun sing - et und seid froh!
Let us our hom - age shew,
A. 2
f
In dul - ci ju - bi - lo
Nun
Let
T. 2
f
In dul - ci ju - bi - lo
Nun
Let
B. 1
f
In dul - ci ju - bi - lo
Nun
Let
B. 2
f
In dul - ci ju - bi - lo
Nun
Let
Tpts
f
f

35
S. 1
Nun sing - et und seid froh!
Let us our hom - age shew,
S. 2
Nun sing - et und seid froh!
Let us our hom - age shew,
A. 1
Nun sing - et und seid froh! Nun sing - et
Let us our hom - age shew, let us our
T. 1
Nun sing - et und seid froh! Nun
Let us our hom - age shew, let
A. 2
sing - et und seid froh! Nun sing - et und seid
us our hom - age shew, let us our hom - age
T. 2
sing - et und seid froh! Nun sing - et und seid froh, seid
us our hom - age shew, let us our hom - age shew, let
B. 1
sing - et und seid froh! Nun sing - et und seid froh! Nun sing - et
us our hom - age shew, let us our hom - age shew, let us our
B. 2
sing - et und seid froh! Nun sing - et und seid froh, seid
us our hom - age shew, let us our hom - age shew, let
Tpts
f

43
B
S. 1
Nun sing - et und seid froh, seid froh!
Let us our hom - age shew;
S. 2
mf più legato
Nun sing - et und seid froh! Un - sers Her-zen
Let us our hom - age shew; Our heart's joy re -
A. 1
mf più legato
und seid froh! Nun sing - et und seid froh! Un - sers
hom - age shew, let us our hom - age shew; Our heart's
T. 1
mf più legato
sing - et und seid froh, seid froh! Un - sers
us our hom - age shew, shew; Our heart's
A. 2
froh! Nun sing - et und seid froh!
shew, let us our hom - age shew;
T. 2
froh! Nun sing - et und seid froh!
us, let us our hom - age shew;
B. 1
und seid froh! Nun sing - et und seid froh!
hom - age shew, our hom - age, hom-age shew;
B. 2
froh! Nun sing - et und seid froh!
us, let us our hom - age shew;
Tpts
B Tempo I
mf
più legato

50
mf più legato
S. 1
Un - sers Her-zen Won - ne, un - - sers Her-zen Won -
Our heart's joy re - clin - eth, our heart's joy re - clin -
S. 2
Won - ne, un - sers Her-zen Won - - ne, un - - sers Her-zen
-clin - eth, our heart's joy re - clin - - eth, our heart's joy re -
A. 1
Her - zen Won - ne, un - - sers Her-zen Won - ne, un -
joy re - clin - eth, our heart's joy re - clin - eth, our
T. 1
Her-zen Won - ne, un - sers Her-zen Won - ne, un -
joy re - clin - eth, our heart's joy re - clin - eth, our
A. 2
T. 2
B. 1
B. 2
Tpts

56
S. 1
- ne, un -sers Her-zen Won - - ne,
- eth, our heart's joy re - clin - - eth,
S. 2
Won - ne, Won - - - ne,
- clin - eth, re - clin - - eth,
A. 1
- sers Her - zen Won - - ne,
heart's joy re - clin - - eth,
T. 1
- sers Her-zen Won - - - - - ne,
heart's joy re - clin - - - - - eth,
A. 2
mf legato
Un - sers Her-zen Won - -
Our heart's joy re - clin - -
T. 2
mf legato
Un - sers Her-zen Won - -
Our heart's joy re - clin - -
B. 1
mf legato
Un - sers Her-zen Won - -
Our heart's joy re - clin - -
B. 2
mf legato
Un - sers Her-zen Won - -
Our heart's joy re - clin - -
Tpts

62
S. 1
un - sers Her-zen Won-ne,
our heart's joy re - clin-eth,
S. 2
un - sers Her-zen Won-ne,
our heart's joy re - clin-eth,
A. 1
un - sers Her-zen Won-ne,
our heart's joy re - clin-eth,
T. 1
un - sers Her-zen Won-ne,
our heart's joy re - clin-eth,
A. 2
-ne Leit in prae - se-pi-o, un - sers Her-zen Won - ne,
- eth in prae - se-pi-o, our heart's joy re - clin - eth,
T. 2
-ne Leit in prae - se - pi - o, un - sers Her-zen Won - ne,
- eth in prae - se - pi - o, our heart's joy re - clin - eth,
B. 1
-ne Leit in prae - se - pi - o, un - sers Her-zen Won - ne,
- eth in prae - se - pi - o, our heart's joy re - clin - eth,
B. 2
-ne Leit in prae - se - pi - o, un - sers Her-zen Won - ne,
- eth in prae - se - pi - o, our heart's joy re - clin - eth,
Tpts

C
69
S. 1
S. 2
A. 1
T. 1
A. 2
T. 2
B. 1
B. 2
Tpts
f
un - sers Her - zen Won - - ne
our heart's joy re - clin - - - eth
Leit
In
C

76
S. 1
in prae - se - pi - o, Und leuch - tet als die Son - ne Ma -
prae - se - pi - o, And like a bright star shin - eth
S. 2
in prae - se - pi - o, Und leuch - tet als die Son - ne
prae - se - pi - o, And like a bright star shin - eth
A. 1
in prae - se - pi - o, Und leuch - tet als die Son - ne Ma -
prae - se - pi - o, And like a bright star shin - eth
T. 1
in prae - se - pi - o, Und leuch - tet als die Son - ne Ma - tris in
prae - se - pi - o, And like a bright star shin - eth
A. 2
Und leuch - tet, und leuch - tet als die Son -
And like, and like a bright star shin -
T. 2
Und leuch - tet als die Son - ne Ma -
And like a bright star shin - eth
B. 1
Und leuch - tet als die Son - ne Ma -
And like a bright star shin - eth
B. 2
Und leuch - tet als die Son - ne Ma -
And like a bright star shin - eth
Tpts
f
f

85
S. 1
-tris in gre - mi - - o:
S. 2
Ma - tris in gre - - mi - o:
A. 1
-tris in gre - mi - o, in gre - mi - o:
T. 1
gre - mi - o, in gre - - mi - o:
A. 2
- ne Ma - tris in gre - - mi - o:
- eth
T. 2
- tris in gre - mi - o:
B. 1
-tris in gre - mi - o, in gre - - mi - o:
B. 2
- tris in gre - mi - - o:
Tpts

D
90
mf più marc.
S. 1
Al-pha es et O, Al-pha es et O,
S. 2
Al-pha es et O, Al-pha es et O,
A. 1
Al-pha es et O, Al-pha es et O, Al-pha es et O,
T. 1
Al-pha es et O, Al-pha es et O, Al-pha es et O,
A. 2
Al-pha es et O, Al-pha es et
T. 2
Al-pha es et O,
B. 1
Al-pha es et O,
B. 2
Al-pha es et O,
Tpts
D
mf più marc.

96
S. 1
mf
Al-pha
S. 2
mf
Al-pha
A. 1
mf
Al-pha
T. 1
mf
Al-pha
A. 2
O, Al-pha es et O, Al-pha es et O, Al-pha es et O,
T. 2
Al-pha es et O, Al-pha es et O, Al - pha es et O,
B. 1
Al-pha es et O, Al-pha es et O, Al - - pha es et O,
B. 2
Al-pha es et O, Al-pha es et O, Al-pha es et O,
Tpts

102
S. 1
es et O, Al-pha es et O,
S. 2
es et O, Al-pha es et O,
A. 1
es et O, Al-pha es et O,
T. 1
es et O, Al-pha es et O,
A. 2
Al-pha es et O, Al-pha es et O, Al - pha es et O,
T. 2
Al-pha es et O, Al - pha es et O, Al - pha
B. 1
Al-pha es et O, Al-pha es et O, Al - pha es et O,
B. 2
Al-pha es et O, Al-pha es et O, Al - pha es et O,
Tpts

E
108
S. 1
S. 2
A. 1
T. 1
A. 2
T. 2
B. 1
B. 2
Tpts
f ben marc.
Al - pha es et O,
Al - pha es et O, Al-pha
Al - pha es et O,
Al - pha es et O,
Al-pha es et O,
es et O, es et O,
Al - pha es et O,
Al - pha
f
E

115
S. 1
ff
Al - pha es et O, Al - pha es et
S. 2
es et O, Al - pha es et
A. 1
ff
Al - pha es et O, Al - pha es et
T. 1
ff
Al - pha es et O, Al - pha es et
A. 2
ff
es et O, Al - pha es et O, Al - pha es et
T. 2
ff
es et O, Al - pha es et
B. 1
ff
es et O, Al - pha es et
B. 2
ff
es et O, Al - pha es et
Tpts
ff
ff
ff

120
S. 1
O.
S. 2
O.
A. 1
O.
T. 1
O.
A. 2
O.
T. 2
O.
(O)
B. 1
O.
B. 2
O.
Tpts

15. Hodie Christus natus est

(*Hear the glad news today*)

Antiphon at Christmas Day Vespers
English translation by John Rutter

J. P. SWEELINCK
(1562–1621)

7
S.
-e, no - e, no - e, no - e.
-well, no - well, no - well, no - well.
Ho - di - e, ho - di - e
Hear the glad news to - day:
no - e, no - e, no - e.
no - well, no - well, no - well.
A.
no - e, no - e.
no - well, no - well.
T.
Ho - di - e, ho - di - e
Hear the glad news to - day:
B.
no - e, no - e.
no - well, no - well.
f
(♭)
7
♮
10
mf leggiero
Sal-va - tor ap - pa - ru - it, Sal - va - tor ap - pa - ru - it,
our Sa - viour on earth ap - peared, our Sa - viour on earth ap - peared,
Sal-va - tor ap - pa - ru - it, Sal - va - tor ap - pa - ru - it, Sal - va - tor ap -
our Sa - viour on earth ap - peared, our Sa - viour on earth ap-peared, our Sa - viour on
Sal - va - tor ap - pa - ru - it,
our Sa - viour on earth ap - peared,
Sal - va - tor ap - pa - ru -
our Sa - viour on earth ap -
Sal-va - tor ap - pa - ru - it, Sal - va - tor ap - pa - ru - it, ap - pa - ru -
our Sa - viour on earth ap - peared, our Sa - viour on earth ap - peared, on earth ap -
Sal - va - tor ap - pa -
our Sa - viour on earth
mf

13
S.
Sal - va - tor ap - pa - ru - it, Sal - va - tor ap - pa - ru - it, al - le -
our Sa - viour on earth ap - peared, our Sa - viour on earth ap - peared,
- pa - ru - it, ap - pa - ru - it, Sal - va - tor ap - pa - ru - it, al - le -
earth ap - peared, on earth ap - peared, our Sa - viour on earth ap - peared,
A.
- it, Sal - va - tor ap - pa - ru - it, al - le - lu - ia, al -
- peared, our Sa - viour on earth ap - peared,
T.
- it, Sal - va - tor ap - pa - ru - it, al - le - lu - ia,
- peared, our Sa - viour on earth ap - peared,
B.
- ru - it, Sal - va - tor ap - pa - ru - it, al - le - lu - ia,
ap - peared, our Sa - viour on earth ap - peared,
6♮
16
f
- lu - ia, al - le - lu - ia, al - le - lu - ia, al - le - lu - ia.
- lu - ia, al - le - lu - ia, al - le - lu - ia, al - le - lu - ia, al - le - lu - ia.
- le - lu - ia, al - le - lu - ia, al - le - lu - ia, al - le - lu - ia.
al - le - lu - ia, al - le - lu - ia, al - le - lu - ia, al - le - lu - ia.
al - le - lu - ia, al - le - lu - ia, al - le - lu - ia, al - le - lu - ia.
6/4
♮ 6 6 6

19
S.
f
mp
Ho - di - e, ho - di - e in ter - ra ca - - - nunt an - ge-
Hear the glad news to - day: an - gels are sing - - - ing o'er the
f
mp
mp
Ho - di - e, ho - di - e in ter - ra, in
Hear the glad news to - day: an - gels are
A.
f
mp
Ho - di - e, ho - di - e in ter - ra
Hear the glad news to - day: an - gels are
T.
f
mp
Ho - di - e, ho - di - e in ter - ra ca - - - nunt an - ge-
Hear the glad news to-day: an - gels are sing - - - ing o'er the
B.
f
mp
Ho - di - e, ho - di - e in ter - ra
Hear the glad news to - day: an-gels
f
mp
23
S.
cresc.
-li, in ter - ra ca - - - - nunt an - ge -
earth, are sing - ing, sing - - - - ing o'er the
cresc.
ter - ra, in ter - ra ca - - - nunt an - ge - li, in ter - ra ca-nunt an - ge -
sing - ing, are sing - ing, sing - - - ing o'er the earth, an - gels are sing-ing o'er the
A.
cresc.
ca - - - nunt an - ge - li, in ter - ra ca-nunt an - ge - li, in ter - ra ca-nunt an - ge -
sing - - - ing o'er the earth, an - gels are sing-ing o'er the earth, an - gels are sing-ing o'er the
T.
cresc.
-li, in ter - ra ca - - nunt an - - - ge - li, ca - - nunt an - ge -
earth, an - gels are sing - - ing o'er the earth, sing - - ing o'er the
B.
in ter - ra ca - - - nunt an - ge - li,
an - gels are sing - - - ing o'er the earth,
cresc.
6♮

26
S.
A.
T.
B.
mf
- li, lae-tan-tur ar-chan - ge - li, lae-tan - tur ar - chan - ge - li, lae - tan-tur ar -
earth, arch-an-gels on high re-joice, arch-an - gels on high re-joice, arch - an- gels on
-li, lae-tan-tur ar-chan - ge- li, lae-tan -tur ar-chan - ge- li, ar -
earth, arch-an-gels on high re-joice, arch-an - gels on high re - joice, on
- li, lae-tan-tur ar-chan - ge - li, lae - tan-tur ar-chan - ge - li, lae-tan-tur ar-chan - ge - li, lae-
earth, arch-an-gels on high re-joice, arch - an-gels on high re - joice, arch-an - gels on high re - joice, arch-
- li, lae-tan-tur ar - chan - ge - li, lae - tan-tur ar-chan - ge - li, lae - tan - tur ar -
earth, arch-an-gels on high re-joice, arch - an- gels on high re - joice, arch - an - gels on
lae-tan-tur ar-chan - ge - li, lae-tan - tur ar - chan - ge - li,
arch-an-gels on high re-joice, arch-an- gels on high re-joice,
6♮ 6♮ 6 ♯ 6 ♯
31
cresc.
-chan - ge - li, ar - chan - ge - li, no - e, no - e, no - e, no - e, no - e, no-
high re - joice, on high re - joice, no - well, no - well, no - well, no - well, no - well, no -
-chan - ge - li, ar - chan - ge - li, no - e, no - e, no - e, no - e, no-
high re - joice, on high re - joice, no - well, no - well, no - well, no - well, no -
-tan - tur ar - chan - ge - li, no - e, no - e, no - e, no-
-an - gels on high re - joice, no - well, no - well, no - well, no -
-chan - ge - li, no - e, no - e, no - e, no - e, no - e, no-
high re - joice, no - well, no - well, no - well, no - well, no - well, no -
lae - tan - tur ar - chan - ge - li, no - e, no - e, no - e, no - e, no-
arch - an - gels on high re - joice, no - well, no - well, no - well, no - well, no -
6 ♮ ♮ ♮ ♮ ♮

35
S.
- e, no - e, no - e, no - e. Ho - di - e, ho - di - e ex - sul - tant ju - sti,
- well, no - well, no - well, no - well. Hear the glad news to - day: sing and be joy - ful,
- e, no - e, no - e, no - e. Ho - di - e, ho - di - e ex - sul - tant ju - sti,
- well, no - well, no - well, no - well. Hear the glad news to - day: sing and be joy - ful,
A.
- e, no - e, no - e. Ho - di - e, ho - di - e ex - sul - tant ju - sti,
- well, no - well, no - well. Hear the glad news to - day: sing and be joy - ful,
T.
- e, no - e, no - e, no - e. Ho - di - e, ho - di - e ex - sul - tant ju - sti,
- well, no - well, no - well, no - well. Hear the glad news to - day: sing and be joy - ful,
B.
- e, no - e, no - e, no - e. Ho - di - e, ho - di - e
- well, no - well, no - well, no - well. Hear the glad news to - day:
f
(f)
[𝄐]
6
39
S.
ex - sul - tant ju - sti, di - cen - tes: glo - ri - a,
sing and be joy - ful, ye right - eous: glo - ry to God,
ex - sul - tant ju - sti, di - cen - tes: glo - ri - a, glo -
sing and be joy - ful, ye right - eous: glo - ry to God, glo -
A.
ex - sul - tant ju - sti, di - cen - tes: glo - ri - a, glo -
sing and be joy - ful, ye right - eous: glo - ry to God, glo -
T.
ex - sul - tant ju - sti, di - cen - tes: glo - ri - a,
sing and be joy - ful, ye right - eous: glo - ry to God,
B.
ex - sul - tant ju - sti, di - cen - tes: glo - ri - a,
sing and be joy - ful, ye right - eous: glo - ry to God,
dim.
mp
6

44
S.
glo - ri - a in ex-cel-sis De - o, in ex-cel-sis De - -
glo - ry to God in the high-est hea - vens, in the high-est hea - -
- ri - a in ex-cel-sis De - o, in ex-cel-sis De - o, in ex-cel-sis De -
- ry to God in the high-est hea - vens, in the high-est hea - vens, in the high-est hea -
A.
- ri - a in ex-cel-sis De - - - o, in ex-cel-sis De - o, in ex-
- ry to God in the high-est hea - - - vens, in the high-est hea - vens, in the
T.
glo - - - - - ri - a in ex-cel-sis De - o, in ex-cel-sis
glo - - - - - ry to God in the high-est hea - vens, in the high-est
B.
glo - - - - - ri - a in ex-cel-sis De - o, in ex-cel-sis De - -
glo - - - - - ry to God in the high-est hea - vens, in the high-est hea - -
48
S.
cresc.
mf
- - o, glo - - - - - - ri - a in
- - vens, glo - - - - - - ry to God in
cresc.
mf
- - o, glo - - - - - - ri - a, glo - - ri -
- - vens, glo - - - - - - ry to God, glo - - ry to
A.
cresc.
mf
-cel - sis De - o, glo - - ri - a, glo - - - -
high-est hea - vens, glo - - ry to God, glo - - - -
T.
cresc.
mf
De - - o, glo - ri - a, glo - - - - - - ri - a
hea - - vens, glo - ry to God, glo - - - - - - ry to God
B.
cresc.
mf
- o, glo - - - - - - - ri - a, glo - - - -
-vens, glo - - - - - - - ry to God, glo - - - -
cresc.
mf

52
cresc.
f
S.
ex-cel-sis De - o, in ex-cel-sis De - o, al-le-lu-ia, no-
the high-est hea - vens, in the high-est hea-vens, al - le- lu- ia, no-
cresc.
f
- a in ex-cel-sis De - o, De - o, al-le-lu-ia,
God in the high-est hea - vens, hea - vens, al-le-lu-ia,
A.
cresc.
f
- ri - a in ex-cel-sis De - o, al-le-lu-ia, al-le-lu-ia,
- ry to God in the high-est hea - vens, al-le-lu-ia, al-le-lu-ia,
T.
mf cresc.
f
in ex-cel-sis De - o, in ex-cel-sis De - o, al-le-lu-ia, no-
in the high-est hea - vens, in the high-est hea - vens, al-le-lu-ia, no-
B.
cresc.
f
- ri - a in ex-cel-sis De - o, in ex-cel-sis De - o, al-le-lu-ia,
- ry to God in the high-est hea - vens, in the high-est hea-vens, al-le-lu-ia,
cresc.
f
6 6 5 6 5 6 5
56
S.
- e, no - e, no - e, al - le - lu - ia, no - e, no - e, no - e, al - le - lu - ia,
- well, no - well, no - well, al - le - lu - ia, no - well, no - well, no - well, al - le - lu - ia,
al - le - lu - ia, al - le - lu - ia, al - le - lu - ia, no -
al - le - lu - ia, al - le - lu - ia, al - le - lu - ia, no -
A.
al - le - lu - ia, al - le - lu - ia, no - e, no - e, no - e, al - le - lu - ia, no -
al - le - lu - ia, al - le - lu - ia, no - well, no - well, no - well, al - le - lu - ia, no -
T.
- e, no - e, no - e, al - le - lu - ia, al - le - lu - ia, al - le - lu - ia,
- well, no - well, no - well, al - le - lu - ia, al - le - lu - ia, al - le - lu - ia,
B.
al - le - lu - ia, al - le - lu - ia, al - le - lu - ia, al - le - lu - ia,
al - le - lu - ia, al - le - lu - ia, al - le - lu - ia, al - le - lu - ia,
6
♮

59
S.
no - e, no - e, no - e, al - le - lu - ia, no - e, no - e, no-
no - well, no - well, no - well, al - le - lu - ia, no - well, no - well, no-
- e, no - e, no - e, no - e, no - e, no - e, no - e, no - e, no - e, no-
- well, no - well, no - well, no - well, no - well, no - well, no - well, no - well, no - well, no-
A.
- e, no - e, no - e, no - e, no - e, no - e, al - le - lu - ia, al - le - lu - ia, no-
- well, no - well, no - well, no - well, no - well, no - well, al - le - lu - ia, al - le - lu - ia, no-
T.
no - e, no - e, no - e, al - le - lu - ia, al - le - lu-
no - well, no - well, no - well, al - le - lu - ia, al - le - lu-
B.
no - e, no - e, no - e, no - e, no - e, no - e, al - le - lu-
no - well, no - well, no - well, no - well, no - well, no - well, al - le - lu-
♮ 6♮ 6 6 6 6
62
ff
S.
- e, al - le - lu - ia, no - e, no - e, no - e, no - e, no - e, no - e, no - e.
- well, al - le - lu - ia, no - well, no - well, no - well, no - well, no - well, no - well, no - well.
ff
- e, no - e, no - e, al - le - lu - ia, no - e, no - e, no - e, no - e, no - e, no - e.
- well, no - well, no - well, al - le - lu - ia, no - well, no - well, no - well, no - well, no - well, no - well.
A.
ff
- e, no - e, no - e, al - le - lu - ia, no - e, no - e, no - e, no - e, no - e, no - e.
- well, no - well, no - well, al - le - lu - ia, no - well, no - well, no - well, no - well, no - well, no - well.
T.
ff
- ia, no - e, no - e, no - e, no - e, no - e, no - e.
- ia, no - well, no - well, no - well, no - well, no - well, no - well.
B.
ff
- ia, no - e, no - e, no - e, no - e, no - e, no - e.
- ia, no - well, no - well, no - well, no - well, no - well, no - well.
ff
6

16. O magnum mysterium

(*O great mystery divine*)

Matin Responsory for Christmas Day
English translation by John Rutter

T. L. de VICTORIA
(1548–1611)

12
my - - - ste - - ri - um et ad - mi - ra - bi - le, et
- - - - - ste - ry di - vine and won - drous sa - cra - ment, and
my - ste - - ri - um et ad - mi - ra - bi - le sa - cra - men - - tum, et
- ste - ry di - vine and won - drous sa - cra - ment O most ho - - ly, and
et ad - mi - ra - bi - le sa - cra - men - - - - - - - tum, et
and won - drous sa - cra - ment O most ho - - - - - - - - ly, and
my - ste - ri - um et ad - mi - ra - bi - le sa - cra - men - tum, et
- ste - ry di - vine and won - drous sa - cra - ment O most ho - ly, and
poco cresc.
mp
17
ad - mi - ra - bi - le sa - cra - men - tum, ut a - ni - ma - li - a vi -
won - drous sa - cra - ment O most ho - - ly, that in a hum - ble crib the
ad - mi - ra - bi - le sa - cra - men - tum, ut a - ni - ma - li - a vi -
won - drous sa - cra - ment O most ho - ly, that in a hum - ble crib the
ad - mi - ra - bi - le sa - cra - men - tum, ut a - ni - ma - li - a, ut a - ni - ma - li - a vi -
won - drous sa - cra - ment O most ho - ly, that in a hum - ble crib, that in a hum - ble crib the
ad - mi - ra - bi - le sa - cra - men - tum, ut a - ni - ma - li - a vi -
won - drous sa - cra - ment O most ho - ly, that in a hum - ble crib the
dim.
p dolce

23
-de - rent Do - mi - num na - tum, vi - de - rent Do - mi - num na - - -
ox and ass should see their Lord, should see their Lord and their Sa - - -
-de - rent Do - mi - num na - tum, vi - de - rent Do - mi - num na - - - -
ox and ass should see their Lord, should see their Lord and their Sa - - - -
-de - rent Do - mi - num na - - tum, vi - de - rent Do - mi - num na - tum
ox and ass should see their Lord, should see their Lord and their Sa - viour
-dc - rcnt Do - mi - num na - tum ja -
ox and ass should see their Lord be -
cresc.
mf
28
- tum ja - cen - tem in prae - se - - pi -
- viour be - fore them in hu - man form re -
-tum ja - cen - - - tem, ja - cen - tem in prae - se -
-viour be - fore them, be - fore them in hu - man form
ja - cen - tem in prae - se - - - - - pi - o, ja -
be - fore them in hu - man form re - vealed, be -
-cen - tem in prae - se - - - - pi - o, ja - cen -
-fore them in hu - man form re - vealed, be - fore

33
- o, ja - cen - tem in prae - se - -
- vealed, be - fore them in hu - man form
- - pi - o, ja - cen - tem in prae - - - se - -
re - vealed, be - fore them in hu - man form
- cen - tem in prae - se - - - - - pi - o, in prae - se - -
- fore them in hu - - - - - man form, in hu - man form
- tem in prae - se - - - - - pi - o, in prae - se - -
them in hu - man form re - vealed, in hu - man form
cresc.
mf
38
- - pi - o: O be - a - ta Vir - - - - -
re - vealed: O most bless - ed Vir - - - - -
- - pi - o: O be - a - ta Vir - - - - -
re - vealed: O most bless - ed Vir - - - - -
- - pi - o: O be - a - ta Vir - - - - -
re - vealed: O most bless - ed Vir - - - - -
- - pi - o: O be - a - ta Vir - - - - -
re - vealed: O most bless - ed Vir - - - - -
p
pp

* $\Phi\frac{3}{2}$ in source. Note values quartered in this section.

55
-ia, al - le - lu - ia, al - le - lu - ia, al - le - lu - ia, al -
-ia, al - le - lu - ia, al - le - lu - ia, al - le - lu - ia, al - le - lu -
-ia, al - le - lu - ia, al - le - lu - ia, al - le - lu - ia, al - le - lu -
Al - le - lu - ia, al - le - lu - ia, al - le - lu -
f
63
-le - lu - ia, al - le - lu - ia, al - le -
-ia, al - le - lu - ia, al - le - lu - ia, al - le - lu -
-ia, al - le - lu - ia, al - le - lu - ia, al - le - lu -
-ia, al - le - lu - ia, al - le - lu - ia, al - le -
69
- lu - ia.
- ia, al - le - lu - ia.
- ia, al - le - lu - ia.
- lu - ia, al - le - lu - ia.
mf
mp

COMMENTARY

Notes

1. Specific references to musical notes in the scores are given thus: bar number (Arabic), stave number counting down from the top stave in each system (Roman), symbol number in the bar (Arabic). For example, in the Bruckner *Virga Jesse floruit*, 6 iii 2 refers to the tenor G♯ in bar 6.
2. Pitch and rhythmic references are given in terms of the editions in this book, not in terms of the original sources. Where editions are transposed and note values shortened, so are all references to variants.

1. Bruckner: *Virga Jesse floruit*

By the time Bruckner wrote this eloquent *a cappella* setting in 1885 he had moved on from his origins as a provincial organist-composer in Linz and was living in Vienna, devoting most of his energy to symphonic writing. Like all his later church music, however, *Virga Jesse floruit* is a carefully considered and significant piece. It was written for the centenary celebrations of the diocese of Linz and published along with *Christus factus est*, *Locus iste*, and *Os justi* as one of a set of four graduals, though strictly speaking its text is an alleluia verse rather than a gradual. *Source:* first edition (Rättig, Vienna, 1886, published as no. 4 of *Vier Graduale*). *Variants:* 61: all voices have 'imo', amended here to accord with the *Liber Usualis* / 63 i 4: tie to the first note of next bar absent in source.

2. Byrd: *O magnum mysterium* and *Beata Virgo*

Byrd has long presented a puzzle to scholars because so much of his large output of church music was written in Protestant England for the forbidden Catholic liturgy, and was openly published in his lifetime without the renowned but recusant composer apparently incurring any penalty for it. He may have been protected by the patronage of the Catholic nobleman Lord Petre, the dedicatee of Vol. II of the *Gradualia* (a collection of 109 motets and related liturgical pieces, from which the present pair of motets is taken), at whose country house in Essex clandestine Catholic worship using Byrd's music very likely took place. *O magnum mysterium* and *Beata Virgo* are nos. 8 and 9 of the 46 motets in Vol. II; they are designated as 'In nativitate Domini' [for the Lord's nativity]. *Source: Gradualia Lib. Secundus* (London, 1610, reissue of original 1607 edition). *Variants:* Spellings in source, 'misterium' and 'visera' have been amended to accord with the *Liber Usualis* / 51–2: the word 'meruerunt', missing in all voices, has been supplied from the *LU*.

3. Cui: *Magnificat* (*Vyelichit dusha moya Gospoda*), op. 93

This exceptionally fine canticle setting, its verses interspersed according to Russian Orthodox usage with a refrain taken from the Hymn to the Virgin, is one of Cui's comparatively few sacred works. In its fervent, almost operatic text-setting, its wide-ranging harmonies, and above all in its rich and sonorous choral texture, it stands on a level with the finest of Tchaikovsky's and Rachmaninov's church music. Cui, born in Vilnius of mixed Lithuanian and French descent, studied engineering in St Petersburg, which became his lifelong home. Engineering remained his profession (he was an expert on military fortifications), but he composed prolifically and was also active as a critic, gaining prominence as one of 'The Five', also known as 'The Mighty Handful'—a group of composers led by Balakirev which sought to establish a distinctively Russian school of composition. Cui's efforts centred mainly around opera, but he had more success with his songs and piano pieces. He wrote the *Magnificat* when he was semi-retired. It was printed by the Imperial Court Chapel in St Petersburg, and may therefore have been commissioned for the Court Chapel Choir. *Source:* first edition (St Petersburg, 1914), score and voice parts.

4. Dering: *Quem vidistis, pastores?*

Like his contemporary Peter Philips, Richard Dering was an English Catholic musician who went into exile in the Spanish Netherlands (or, according to another account, converted to Catholicism while visiting Rome in 1612). By 1617 he was organist to the convent of English nuns in Brussels, and in the same year issued his *Cantiones Sacrae*; the publisher was the noted Phalèse of Antwerp who also published music by Philips. *Quem vidistis, pastores?*, one of Dering's best-known motets, comes from a second collection, the six-voiced *Cantica Sacra* of 1618. The inclusion of a *basso continuo* is just one sign of the new Italian baroque style which composers in England were slower to embrace. Dering brings the dialogue between the earthly shepherds and their (perhaps) heavenly interlocutors vividly to life by dividing the choir into two halves, high and low, all voices eventually joining in a joyful cascade of alleluias. *Source: Cantica Sacra ad melodiam madrigalium elaborata senis vocibus Cum basso continuo ad Organum* (Antwerp, 1618) *Variant:* 32 iv 2: B in source, amended here to accord with the continuo bass.

5. Flecha the elder (*attrib.*): *Riu, riu, chiu*

This tuneful and spirited piece first appeared in *Villancicos de diversos autores*, a collection of Spanish polyphonic songs published, without names of authors or composers, in 1556. The traditional ascription to Mateo Flecha the elder appears to be based only on the fact that he was a leading Spanish composer of the time who wrote a number of other vernacular polyphonic Christmas pieces, the so-called *ensaladas*, which are stylistically similar, though longer. The *villancico* was a Spanish musical and poetic form akin to the Italian *ballata*, characterized by a patterned alternation of verse and refrain. Originally secular, by the sixteenth century it was used for sacred vernacular pieces, and became especially associated with Christmas. The phrase 'riu, riu, chiu' was a traditional call of Spanish shepherds guarding their flocks. The present edition gives nos. 1, 2, 3, and 7 of the original seven verses. *Source: Villancicos de diversos autores* (Venice, 1556). Original clefs SATB, original time signature C, original pitch a tone lower. Note values have been halved and barlines inserted. In the source, verses after the first one are printed separately, not underlaid to the notes; their underlay in the present edition is editorial.

6. Handl: *Resonet in laudibus*

Jacob Handl (sometimes known as Gallus) was born in Slovenia. In his youth he left his homeland, becoming a singer at the Imperial chapel in Vienna. In 1575 he embarked upon further travels, then in 1580 became choirmaster to the Bishop of Olomouc, settling finally in Prague in 1586 as director of music at the church of St Jan. His compositions, mainly vocal, were highly regarded in his own day. Handl published most of them himself: there are four books of motets, arranged according to the church's year. *Resonet in laudibus*, taken from Vol. I of these, is a slightly elaborated version of a famous German carol melody believed to date from the fourteenth century. The same melody was (and still is) equally popular to the German words 'Joseph, lieber Joseph mein', a cradle song. *Source: Tomus primus Operis Musici Cantionum . . . Jacopo Handl* (Prague, 1586). Original clefs C1, C2, C3, F3, original time signature ¢ 3, note values divided by eight, original pitch unaltered. Choirs I and II are indicated by the word 'alternatim', full choir by 'Totus chorus'.

7. Handl: *Omnes de Saba venient*

This resplendent Epiphany motet, which seems to move with the majestic tread of a royal procession, comes from the first volume of Handl's *Opus Musicum*. The text is the Gradual for the Feast of the Epiphany. *Source:* as for no. 6. *Variants:* 5 iv 4: D in source / 19–20 iii: F ♩ G 𝅗𝅥, amended to avoid parallel fifths with the soprano / 21 iv 2: D ♪ (no C), an unlikely dissonance unless followed by C to create a pair of passing notes. The editorial amendment makes a more exact parallel with the soprano in bar 27.

8. Mendelssohn: *Frohlocket, ihr Völker auf Erden*, op. 79 no.1

In 1840 Friedrich Wilhelm IV, the new king of Prussia, asked Mendelssohn to be head of an Academy of the Arts in Berlin. One of Mendelssohn's duties was to conduct a newly formed Berlin cathedral choir, and during his tenure of office from 1843 (which ended prematurely in 1844 as a result of disputes and frustrations) he wrote a number of sacred pieces for the choir. Op. 79 is a set of six unaccompanied eight-voiced *Sprüche* published posthumously in 1848. *Spruch*, in a religious context, means a short but significant biblical or liturgical text; 'sentence' is the closest English equivalent. Mendelssohn took the texts of all six op. 79 settings from the seasonal appendix to Berlin Cathedral's own prayer book, the *Kirchen-Agende für die Hof- und Domkirche in Berlin* (Berlin, 1822). *Frohlocket, ihr Völker auf Erden*, written in 1843, uses eight-voiced writing for richly sonorous rather than antiphonal or contrapuntal effect. *Source: Werke*, ed. Rietz, Vol. xiv.

9. Mouton: *Nesciens mater*

This celebrated motet, of heart-easing tranquillity and beauty, first appeared in the Medici Codex of 1518, a sumptuously illuminated manuscript collection of motets reputedly copied under Mouton's direction as a wedding gift for Lorenzo de' Medici and his young French bride. Mouton was a French priest-musician, who, after various provincial appointments including choirmastership at Amiens Cathedral, entered the service of the French court as composer and attained widespread fame: over half of his 100 or so motets and 15 masses were published in his lifetime. He was renowned for his effortless contrapuntal skill, to which *Nesciens mater* bears witness: its smooth, flowing eight-voiced polyphony is produced by four voices (the tenor based on a chant), which are imitated by four more following them at four beats' distance and a fifth higher. So strict is the quadruple canon that only the four 'leading' voices appear in the manuscript, the others being deduced from them. This technique could have been suggested to Mouton by the text, which speaks of the Virgin bringing forth a child without pain, just as his four voices 'bring forth' four more. *Source:* Medici Codex (1518). Also consulted: *Treize livres de motets parus chez Pierre Attaignant en 1534 et 1535*, ed. Smijers and Merritt, Vol. iii. See Lowinsky, *The Medici Codex of 1518* (*Monuments of Renaissance Music,* Chicago, 1968) for a full discussion of the chant derivation of the tenor part and questions of text underlay.

10. Palestrina: *Hodie Christus natus est*

Palestrina's life and work centred around Rome. In 1551 he was appointed *maestro* of the Cappella Giulia, the choir of St Peter's Basilica; periods of directorship at the churches of St John Lateran (1555–60) and S. Maria Maggiore (1561–6) were followed by a return in 1571 to the Cappella Giulia, where he remained till his death. His stream of publications began with a book of madrigals in 1555; eventually there were seven books of masses, six of motets, and sundry other volumes of liturgical music and madrigals. *Hodie Christus natus est* was published in 1575. In its rhythmically clear-cut antiphonal exchanges between high and low choirs, and its voice writing which is more chordal and less contrapuntal than is usual with Palestrina, it prefigures the slightly later Venetian style of Giovanni Gabrieli. The joyous mood of the text is memorably captured, and, as with other Christmas motets of the period, 'alleluia' is replaced by 'noe, noe'. *Source: Motettorum liber tertius* (Venice, 1575).

11. Philips: *O beatum et sacrosanctum diem*

Peter Philips, together with Richard Dering, stands apart from the illustrious group of English composers of his period, by reason of exile. After childhood and youth in London as a choirboy at St Paul's Cathedral, Philips (who was firmly Catholic) fled to the continent in 1582. After various European travels, he settled in Antwerp, where he pursued a successful career as composer and teacher, later moving to Brussels where he was chapel organist to the Archduke Albert. Philips's musical contacts being more with his continental contemporaries than his compatriots, it is not surprising that his motets (most of which were published in his lifetime) are often more like Monteverdi than Byrd: dramatic, sectional, and concise, filled with contrasts rather than with counterpoint. *O beatum et sacrosanctum diem*, from his *Cantiones Sacrae* of 1612, is a jubilant setting of its Christmas text—the model, perhaps, for Sweelinck's better-known *Hodie Christus natus est*. *Source: Cantiones Sacrae . . . quinis vocibus* (Phalèse, Antwerp, 1612).

12. H. Praetorius: *In dulci jubilo*

Hieronymus Praetorius—no relation of his better-known compatriot and contemporary Michael Praetorius—was one of a dynasty of Hamburg organist-composers. From 1586 until his death he was organist at the church of St Jacobi, composing a substantial quantity of church music, most of which was published in his lifetime in a five-volume edition. *In dulci jubilo* is one of two carol settings (the other being *Joseph, lieber Joseph mein*) appended to an eight-voiced Magnificat first published in 1602, a custom also followed by Bach with the Christmas interpolations in his E flat Magnificat of 1723. The double-choir layout of the voices is typical of Praetorius's predilection for Venetian polychoral style, a novelty in Germany at that time. *Source: Cantiones Sacrae . . . ab Hieronymo Prætorio Sen.* (Hamburg, 1622 reprint of 1602 edition). *Variants:* 2–3: all voices have 'nu' instead of 'nun' / 3: Choir II voices have 'singt und weset froh' / 25: the word 'da' has been editorially inserted to make up a seven-syllable line consistent with the earlier stanzas.

13. M. Praetorius: *Quem pastores laudavere*

Born to a Lutheran family in Creuzberg, a small town not far from Bach's birthplace, Eisenach, Michael Praetorius became one of the leading composers, organists, and music theorists of the German-speaking lands, despite being largely self-taught in music. He held various church and court posts, notably in Wolfenbüttel, Kassel, and Dresden, and published an impressive quantity of music, of which over 1000 pieces were intended for the Lutheran liturgy, ranging from simple two-part hymns to complex polychoral motets. Amidst this huge and still largely unexplored output is some singularly attractive Christmas music, of which *Quem pastores laudavere* is a charming example. Praetorius made several settings of this familiar carol. The present one, published in 1607, has alternative Latin and German versions of the text. At the end of each stanza, Praetorius quotes another well-known carol, *Resonet in laudibus* (see no. 6 in this volume). Verse 3 of the opening section (to bar 16) is here omitted, as is verse 4 of bars 17–52. The optional organ accompaniment in bars 1–16 is taken from a later setting of the tune (in Praetorius's *Puericinium* collection of 1621): in the 1607 version, bars 1–16 are left unaccompanied. *The New Oxford Book of Carols* draws attention to the German custom of singing this melody *in Wechsel*, that is, by four boys holding candles, placed in high galleries around the church, so that 'the tune seems to revolve in the air, as if sung by circling angels' (*NOBC*, p. 189). *Sources: Musae Sioniae*, Vol. v (Wolfenbüttel, 1607) and *Puericinium* (Frankfurt, 1621). Original clefs SATB, original time signature **C3**, note values quartered, original pitch a tone lower. *Variant:* 10–11 i: 'resonat', amended to accord with familiar *NOBC* version.

14. Scheidt: *In dulci jubilo*

The enduring popularity of the medieval German carol upon which this radiantly festive motet is based can be shown by the numerous vocal and instrumental settings of it which have appeared over the centuries. Samuel Scheidt's quite elaborate version, with its two florid parts for *clarini*, first appeared in his *Cantiones Sacrae* (1620), an impressive collection of double-choir motets recognizably German in style but influenced by Scheidt's teacher Sweelinck and by Venetian polychoral technique. It was the first of seven published collections of vocal and instrumental music which Scheidt issued in the course of a career spent mainly as a court and church musician in his native city of Halle. *Source: Cantiones Sacrae octo vocum* (Hamburg, 1620). *Variants:* 101 i 1: E / 101 v 3: ♩

15. Sweelinck: *Hodie Christus natus est*

This sparkling and joyous Christmas motet first appeared in 1619, as one of 37 *Cantiones sacrae* by Sweelinck published in Antwerp, all five-voiced and with Latin texts. It was the composer's only Latin publication: his *magnum opus* was a four-volume collection of polyphonic settings of all 150 psalms in French translations. Sweelinck was organist of the Oude Kerk in Amsterdam and a renowned teacher. An attractive feature of *Hodie Christus natus est* is the appearance of bell-like figures to the word 'noe', replacing some of the customary alleluias. This seasonal touch is found in other Christmas motets of the period (see nos. 10 and 11 in the present volume). The continuo bass mostly follows the lowest sounding vocal part, but occasionally it provides the 'real' bass which is missing in the voice parts (as in bar 56), so clearly *Hodie Christus natus est* was not intended for *a cappella* performance, though it can certainly be done that way. Organ accompaniment (without 16-foot bass) is one possibility, and instrumental doubling of all voice parts, plus a continuo, is also effective. *Source: Cantiones sacrae* (Antwerp, 1619).

16. Victoria: *O magnum mysterium*

Victoria began his musical life as a choirboy at Avila Cathedral, then moved to Rome to study at the Jesuit Collegio Germanico; he may have received tuition from Palestrina. He was made director of music at the Collegio in 1573, and was ordained priest in 1575. In 1576 he joined St Philip Neri's community, later taking chaplaincies at two Roman churches. Despite growing European fame from his compositions (all of them sacred), he wanted to return to a quieter life in Spain, and in 1587 he accepted Philip II's offer to become chaplain to his sister, the Dowager Empress Maria, who lived in retirement at the convent of Descalzas Reales in Madrid. Victoria remained at the convent, first as choirmaster and later as organist, until his death. *O magnum mysterium*, which was included in Victoria's first published collection of 1572, is one of the best-loved of all Christmas motets, a succinct expression of both the mystery and the joy of the Nativity. The composer later based a mass setting on it; this was published in 1592. The text of the motet is proper to Christmas Day Matins, according to the *Liber Usualis*, but in the original publication *O magnum mysterium* is headed 'in circumcisione Domini' (January 1st). *Source: Thomæ Ludovici de Victoria Abulensis motecta . . .* (Rome, 1583: a reprint, with minor alterations, of the motet as it appears in the 1572 publication).